PUB WALKS ALONG
The Pilgrims Way
the North Downs

TWENTY CIRCULAR WALKS

Charles Whynne-Hammond

COUNTRYSIDE BOOKS
NEWBURY, BERKSHIRE

First published 1998
© Charles Whynne-Hammond 1998

Reprinted 2002

COUNTRYSIDE BOOKS
3 Catherine Road
Newbury, Berkshire

ISBN 1 85306 499 8

To view our complete range of books,
please visit us at
www.countrysidebooks.co.uk

Designed by Graham Whiteman
Cover illustration by Colin Doggett
Photographs by the author
Maps by Glenys Jones

Produced through MRM Associates Ltd., Reading
Printed by J. W. Arrowsmith Ltd., Bristol

Contents

Walk

Publisher's Note

We hope that you obtain considerable enjoyment from this book; great care has been taken in its preparation. Although at the time of publication all routes followed public rights of way or permitted paths, diversion orders can be made and permissions withdrawn.

We cannot of course be held responsible for such diversion orders and any inaccuracies in the text which result from these or any other changes to the routes nor any damage which might result from walkers trespassing on private property. We are anxious though that all details covering the walks are kept up to date and would therefore welcome information from readers which would be relevant to future editions.

THE PILGRIMS' WAY AND NORTH DOWNS WAY WINCHESTER TO REIGATE

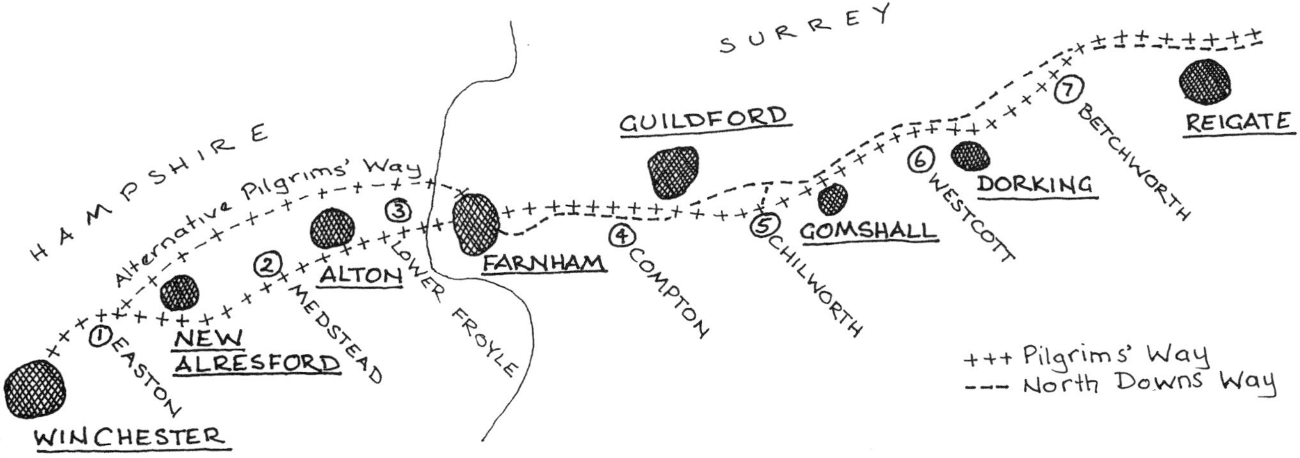

SURREY

REIGATE

⑦ BETCHWORTH

DORKING

⑥ WESTCOTT

GOMSHALL

⑤ SCHILWORTH

GUILDFORD

④ COMPTON

FARNHAM

③ LOWER FROYLE

ALTON

② MEDSTEAD

NEW ALRESFORD

① EASTON

WINCHESTER

HAMPSHIRE

Alternative Pilgrims' Way

+++ Pilgrims' Way
--- North Downs Way

LOCATION OF PUB WALKS 1-7

THE PILGRIMS' WAY AND NORTH DOWNS WAY REIGATE TO WYE

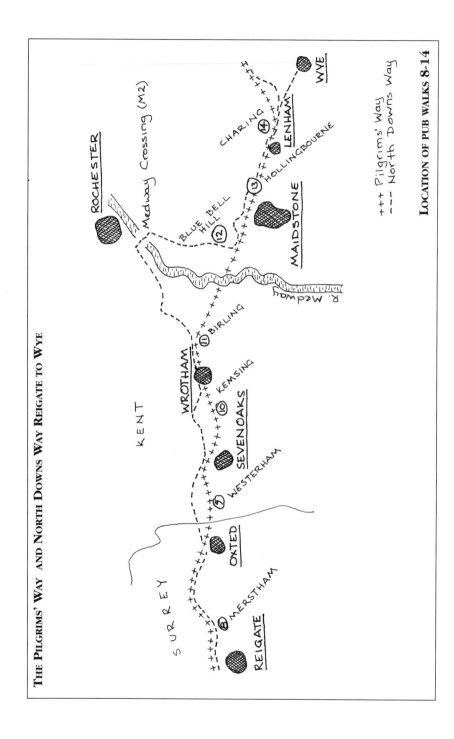

LOCATION OF PUB WALKS 8-14

The Pilgrims' Way & North Downs Way (The Kent Loop) between Wye & the English Channel

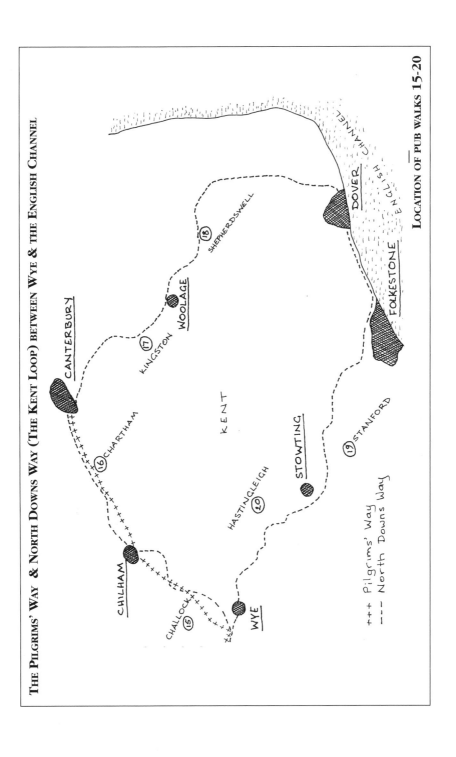

Location of pub walks 15-20

INTRODUCTION

On 29th December 1170 Archbishop Thomas à Becket was murdered in Canterbury Cathedral, four knights hacking him down after hearing the King, Henry II, utter the fatal words, 'Will no one rid me of this turbulent priest?' The Cathedral later became a shrine to the canonised Becket and Canterbury one of the most important centres of pilgrimage in Europe.

Over the next four centuries a network of pilgrim routes developed. One of these led south from London and was immortalised by Geoffrey Chaucer in the *Canterbury Tales*; another led up from the Channel coast, along the North Downs, and was used by pilgrims from abroad. The most famous linked Canterbury with Winchester, which itself held the shrine to St Swithun and was a place of pilgrimage. It was along this route, across southern England, that most pilgrim traffic seems to have taken place, with travellers moving in either direction. However, it was not until much later, long after pilgrimages had ceased, that the name Pilgrims' Way was first adopted for this particular route.

It should be noted, however, that the first pilgrims did not create their own route from scratch. They used existing trackways, paths and roads, linking together those sections which gave the easiest, shortest or cheapest route. For much of the distance a prehistoric trackway was followed, this running along the chalk uplands above the wetter, more forested, vales and valleys. Thus, the Pilgrims' Way crossed the Hampshire Downs from Winchester to Farnham and then contoured along the lower slopes of the North Downs all the way to Canterbury.

Today long sections of the Pilgrims' Way can still be followed, along modern roads, trackways and footpaths. The distance is about 120 miles. However, because of the fact that some parts have been lost, and other parts have been turned to tarmac, the Pilgrims' Way is not actually a designated long distance footpath.

In 1978 the North Downs Way National Trail was officially opened, having been planned by the Countryside Commission in co-operation with Surrey and Kent County Councils. This runs from Farnham to the Channel coast along the line of the chalk escarpment. At its eastern end there is the 'Canterbury' or 'Kent Loop', where the National Trail runs in a circle to link Canterbury, Dover and Folkestone, the 'split' occurring near the village of Wye near Ashford. The total length of the North Downs Way, including the Loop, is about 150 miles.

The North Downs Way runs parallel to the Pilgrims' Way or else accompanies it exactly. Along some stretches the National Trail follows the crest of the hills, giving walkers panoramic views, whilst the Pilgrims' Way follows the foot of the scarp slope, the south-facing steep slope of the North Downs escarpment. It is generally true that the North Downs Way has a more circuitous route than the Pilgrims' Way since it links together already existing public rights of way.

Where possible the walks in this book include lengths where the North Downs Way and Pilgrims' Way run together. When this is not possible the North Downs Way route is used, but even in these cases parts of the Pilgrims' Way may be followed on the outward or return sections. The North Downs Way is waymarked by an acorn symbol and this symbol has been used in the book to denote where the Way meets the circular walk. All the central lengths of the North Downs Way and/or Pilgrims' Way incorporated in the circular walks are described in the same direction (west to east) as far as Wye. The 'Loop' is described in a clockwise direction. Each walk in the book is illustrated by a sketch map, designed to guide you to the starting point and give a simple but accurate idea of the route to be taken. However, for those who like the benefit of detailed maps, the relevant Ordnance Sheet is very much recommended, especially for identifying the main features of the views. The relevant number of the O.S. Landranger series is given within each chapter of the book. All rights of way mentioned should be walkable and readers who find any difficulties should contact the relevant authority which is responsible for maintaining footpaths and bridleways.

Generally pubs still keep 'normal' opening times – 11 am or 11.30 am to 2.30 pm, 6.30 pm or 7 pm to 11 pm. Sunday afternoon opening and, indeed, all-day opening are now becoming common. Most pubs have car parks where walkers may leave their vehicles but it would be polite to ask permission first from the landlords. The food and drink items mentioned in the text are given only as examples. Menus and ales may change with seasons, kitchen staff and brewery contractual arrangements.

I should like to thank all those pub proprietors who supplied me with information. I am also indebted to Glenys Jones for drawing the maps and Gwen Cassell for helping with the final draft.

Charles Whynne-Hammond

EASTON
The Cricketers Inn
✤

From Winchester to New Alresford the Pilgrim's Way followed the river Itchen upstream. Ignoring the more direct route of an ancient hilltop road, medieval pilgrims probably travelled along the north bank of the river. In this way they could visit Hyde Abbey and the churches of Kings Worthy and Itchen Abbas. This walk offers a splendid introduction to the Itchen valley countryside: lush meadows, downland scenery, beautiful villages and, throughout, the sparkling companionship of an unspoilt Hampshire stream. The route is to Itchen Abbas, and back via Avington.

Easton, which is on the south bank of the Itchen, boasts a fine 12th century church (restored in Victorian times), a wonderful collection of ancient cottages (many of which are thatched) and two excellent pubs. The Chestnut Horse, at the eastern end of the village, dates back to Tudor times. It offers a good range of refreshments and is popular with families. The Cricketers Inn, at the village centre, is less ancient but no less hospitable. Indeed, it is an especially friendly place where locals and tourists happily mix to enjoy the best of English traditional food and drink.

The Cricketers is a freehouse which prides itself on the selection of real ales served. These include various beers from regional breweries like Ringwood and Otter as well as some more 'national' brews such as John Smith. The guest beers may vary from time to time but always there is a good range of flavours and strengths. Strongbow and Inche's draught cider and various wines are also offered together with the usual stouts and lagers.

The food selection is equally impressive. From bar snacks like sandwiches (of various fillings, normal, toasted or 'open'), cheese platters and salads to full meals like steak and kidney pie, casseroles and grills, the range is wide and thoughtful. Daily specials, often involving game or fish, are written up on a blackboard and vegetarians can choose such dishes as wild mushroom gateau or vegetable moussaka. A separate restaurant offers a pleasant and quiet eating area away from the jollity of the bar.

As befits its name this popular pub displays an interesting collection of cricketing memorabilia. Around the cluttered walls of the large, open-plan bar room hang numerous pictures and objects relating to our Summer Game. Over the bar counter is a signed cricket bat donated by Hampshire Cricket Club.

'Normal' pub opening times are kept. Telephone: 01962 779353.

- **HOW TO GET THERE:** Easton is just 3 miles north-east of Winchester city centre, close to the M3 motorway. From Junction 9 the A33 leads to the B3047, which runs along the Itchen valley. The village is just south of that road, reached from Martyr Worthy.
- **PARKING:** There is a pub car park and vehicles can also be left elsewhere in the village, provided no obstruction is caused.
- **LENGTH OF THE WALK:** 4 miles. Map OS Landranger 185 Winchester (inn GR 512322). The route is very easy to follow, being clear and well-signposted. Footpaths across fields are used on the outward journey, a quiet country lane on the return.

THE WALK

From the Cricketers Inn car park turn right and walk along the lane northwards away from the village. Those with time and an interest in

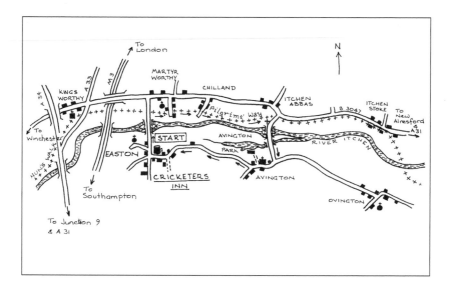

architecture may prefer, first, to visit the church which is reached up Church Lane. It is a fine chateau-style structure with some Norman stonework and ornate archways. The views from the churchyard, across the Itchen meadows, are beautiful, especially to the east which is the direction of the walk.

The route of the Pilgrims' Way is joined across the river Itchen. In medieval times this whole area was open countryside, with villages dotted across the meadow pastures. The present B3047 road probably follows the line of an old packhorse trackway but the pilgrims might not necessarily have kept strictly to this alignment. They are more likely to have chosen the easiest route from church to church, depending upon the ground and river conditions prevailing at any one time.

The footpath to be followed on this walk is signposted immediately beyond the second bridge over the Itchen, coming from Easton. The river divides at this point, close to a brick cottage. Little detailed description is necessary for the path is clearly worn. It runs along the riverbank, past a young woodland, over several stiles, around a paddock and beside some back gardens. The lane at Martyr Worthy is soon reached, where you turn left to reach the church, dedicated to St Swithun. In medieval times, of course, many pilgrims used the Pilgrims' Way westwards, to the Winchester shrine of St Swithun, the bishop and tutor to Alfred the Great.

The route continues along the footpath opposite the church, beside

Easton Lodge.

the village hall. Once again, the way is clear. You will notice yellow arrow discs at intervals, showing the direction, for this path is now part of the locally designated 'Itchen Way'. Through kissing gates you continue, first along a wide grassy track and then along a couple of field edges. Beyond a stile the path bears right descending to the lane at Chilland. Almost opposite the route continues, the direction marked by a footpath signpost. The views along this next stretch are lovely. The river is close by. Beyond some pretty landscaped grounds (private) the countryside opens out to an area of sloping meadows.

As the path climbs slightly, alongside a wooden fence, so the panorama spreads. Across the valley is Avington Park. Beside some back gardens, over a gravel lane and onwards above the meadow pastures, which are down to the right, you will soon reach Itchen Abbas. At the road turn left for the village, right to continue the circular walk.

Itchen Abbas church is a fine Victorian building (on the site of a Norman original) and should be visited. Near an old yew tree in the graveyard lies John Hughes, who was the last man in England to be hanged for horse stealing (in 1823). At the local inn (now called the Trout) Charles Kingsley once stayed. He was the author of *The Water Babies*, a much under-read classic.

The return to Easton is entirely along a road – but a very quiet and pretty road, that runs around the estate of Avington Park. After crossing both bridges over the Itchen and passing the gates to Avington House, keep right at the junction. Avington village boasts some handsome estate cottages, in brick and flint, and one of the most perfect Georgian churches in England (dating from 1770). Avington House itself, seen from a distance, has a grand Classical façade (18th century) but dates originally from Stuart times.

At the far end of Avington village turn right in the direction signposted to Easton. This lane runs attractively past a car park and picnic area (with views across the lake) maintained by Hampshire County Council. Further on, in the woodlands, you pass the elegant Easton Lodge. Easton village itself is soon reached.

Pilgrims' Way

From Winchester to Easton the Pilgrims' Way followed the now designated 'Nuns Walk' from the city outskirts to Kings Worthy. Thereafter it followed the north bank of the Itchen (now passing under the M3). From Itchen Abbas to New Alresford the Pilgrims' Way followed the line of the present B3047 as far as Itchen Stoke. From there, historians think, it crossed the river and entered New Alresford from the south.

MEDSTEAD
The Castle of Comfort

From New Alresford to Alton the Pilgrims' Way continued up the Itchen valley, crossed the watershed and followed the upper reaches of the river Wey. The upland between the two river sources remains well wooded, around the village of Four Marks. In medieval times this area was so forested and wet it created an obstacle to traffic, and for this reason many pilgrims chose an alternative route. Northwards through Old Alresford they joined the prehistoric trackway now called the Oxdrove Way. This led them across open country through Upper Weald and Bentworth. Our circular walk, through Chawton Park Wood, incorporates part of the real Pilgrims' Way. It is a lovely route, especially to be enjoyed for its trees and wildlife.

Medstead is a very long and dispersed village with a wonderful range of architectural styles from Tudor to modern, cottage to mansion. The oldest part is around the church, an attractive Gothic building half-hidden by trees. This stands at the northern edge of the village – as does the Castle of Comfort Inn, which is round the corner.

This is a wonderfully traditional English pub with a cosy, friendly atmosphere and a simple, no-nonsense range of food and drink. The building dates back to the late 17th century. Inside there are two small bar rooms, each with a low ceiling and plain walls nicely cluttered with pictures and horsebrasses. Old wooden furniture and log-burning stoves add charm to the dark, convivial atmosphere. The place is justifiably popular with locals and those travellers who discover it always want to return.

Owned by the Innspired Pub Company, the Castle of Comfort serves Ushers, Courage and selected other real ales. Inche's draught cider and house wines provide alternatives. Food is limited but is well prepared and very reasonably priced. Bar snacks only are offered, these mainly consisting of soup, rolls, ploughman's lunches, sandwiches, 'toasties' and salads. Those requiring a full meal should patronise the large and modernised Windmill Inn on the A31 in Four Marks.

The Castle of Comfort keeps 'normal' pub opening times. Children are welcome: in the garden is a playtime tree house. Telephone: 01420 562112.

- **HOW TO GET THERE:** Medstead is 5 miles north-east of New Alresford and 4 miles south-west of Alton. It is easily reached from the A31, by way of a turning at Four Marks.
- **PARKING:** There is a pub car park. Vehicles can also be left along the village lanes, which are not very busy.
- **LENGTH OF WALK:** 6½ miles. Map OS Landranger 186 Aldershot and Guildford (inn GR 655373). The route is very easy, both to follow and underfoot. A country lane is used to reach the entrance to Chawton Park Wood; a well-marked forest track is used thereafter.

The Walk

From the Castle of Comfort turn right down Castle Street and then left at the junction. This leads past the church to another road junction where there are some shops. Continue straight on down the High Street, followed by Roe Downs Road. Ignore both the right turn (to Soldridge) and the left turn (to Alton). The route runs between the cricket and football pitches and southwards away from the village. Views open out either side across the upper Itchen valley.

In due course turn left at Five Ash Road in the Alton direction. This

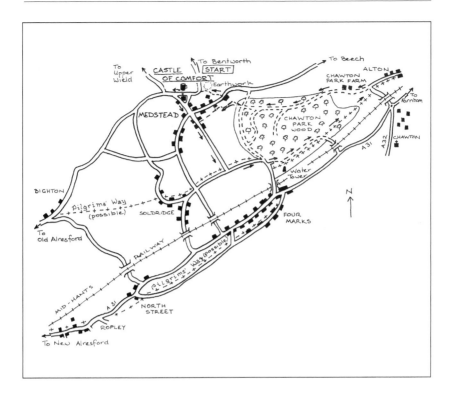

brings you to the entrance to Chawton Park Wood (Forestry Commission). Ignore the bridleway on the left immediately before the notice board. The route continues at the far end of the car park, through a wooden barrier gate.

The Pilgrims' Way, from Four Marks to Alton, crossed the watershed between the Itchen and Wey valleys along an old packhorse road. This ran through a dense, damp woodland area which, at the time of the pilgrims, was infamous for its highwaymen. These thieves may have gone but the line of the road remains.

Beyond the car park turn right towards the water tower enclosure and then left. Route-finding is now easy. A wide straight bridleway runs parallel to a wide straight forest path, these being ten yards apart. Follow either all the way to a group of farm buildings, a distance of about a mile. Beyond these buildings continue in the same direction, now along a single bridleway, this being signposted close to a fence and beyond the point where a gravel track leads down to the right. For a while the bridleway runs alongside a motor cycle track, but soon it

The church at Medstead.

curves quietly through the unspoilt woodland. After another mile or so you reach the edge of the forest and descend to a road at the western extremity of Alton. Turn left and left again, around Chalk Dell Cottages.

For two miles the Pilgrims' Way has been preserved as a woodland track, appropriately since it might have looked rather like this when the pilgrims themselves came this way. Today it is still a lovely walk. Look carefully and you will see the old ditches and embankments either side of the old road. Even in those days it was a very wide thoroughfare. From Tudor to Georgian times the forest supplied timber for the Navy and logs were hauled along this track on horse sledges. For those interested in steam engines, this stretch of the Pilgrims' Way also runs parallel to the Mid-Hants Railway, or the 'Watercress Line'. The preserved section runs from Alresford to Alton and has become a popular tourist attraction.

The return to Medstead begins along the rough tarmac lane to Chawton Park Farm, where deer have been traditionally reared. Beyond the handsome farm buildings this lane becomes a grassy bridleway that runs up a shallow dry valley. Through a wooden bar gate you re-enter Chawton Park Wood and continue straight on. This is another pleasant section. The trees here are pine and not our native deciduous but still the wildlife is active. Follow the wide grassy track as it curves into the distance, keeping right at the next two junctions, after which the way narrows.

In due course a wooden signpost indicates a bridleway left and right and a footpath straight on. Choose the footpath, which takes you to the edge of the woodland. Over the stile here you continue across the middle of a large field. In the far corner cross another stile and bear left. Soon you reach the edge of Medstead village as the clear path leads to more stiles. Turn right up a narrower path that takes you past a large house to the road. There turn right and then, after 100 yards, turn left along another footpath. This is signposted opposite The Oaks Private Road.

The route is now easy. Over several stiles the path crosses a field, runs through a woodland and passes the back of the school. Thereafter it curves round the old earthworks of an Iron Age fort and emerges onto the road. Castle Street, which is opposite, leads to the Castle of Comfort.

Pilgrims' Way

From New Alresford to Four Marks the Pilgrims' Way seems, from historical and topographical evidence, to have used two alternative routes. Perhaps to avoid the damp floor of the upper Itchen valley, one of these routes ran from Bishops Sutton to Ropley and thence south of the present A31, the other ran through the parishes of Bighton and Soldridge. Both these routes kept to slightly higher ground. The line of the modern A31 dual-carriageway, along the valley floor, dates only from the mid 18th century when a turnpike road was constructed.

LOWER FROYLE
The Anchor Inn

From Alton to Farnham the Pilgrims' Way followed the river Wey downstream, probably keeping to the northern side of the valley. Those pilgrims choosing to keep on drier, higher ground would have joined the prehistoric Oxdrove Way north of Alton and travelled through Well village, over the chalk hills to Powderham Castle. This walk accompanies the Pilgrims' Way to Bentley and returns along part of the Oxdrove Way, keeping very much in the footsteps of medieval travellers. The countryside hereabouts is beautiful and the buildings passed have a splendid range of ages and styles. Cameras, sketch pads and artists' easels would be well used.

Upper Froyle is dominated by the Lord Mayor Treloar College, a community for physically handicapped children. The church is an interesting mixture of Gothic features and Georgian red-brick Classical. Lower Froyle is the larger village, having a good collection of Tudor cottages and two pleasant pubs. The Prince of Wales stands at the northern end, the Anchor Inn at the southern end.

The Anchor is said to date from the 15th century, possibly earlier. It certainly has some ancient features, including old oak beams and, in one of the two bar rooms, a deep well. The decor is suitably traditional with brassware and tankards, settles and bench seats, a wooden dado and bare stone walls. In winter months open fires burn in the grates.

This freehouse serves a good selection of real ales (Eldridge Pope, Royal Oak and Thomas Hardy brews), draught cider (Dry Blackthorn), wines (European and New World), stouts and lagers. Menu books list the regular food items (like sandwiches, ploughman's lunches, salads, curries and grills) whilst a large blackboard gives the daily specials. All these dishes are wonderfully cooked, evidently by a chef who takes pride in the buying and preparation of fresh produce. The salmon and steak meals are always excellent and the vegetarian meals are positively mouth-watering – pancakes, nut roasts, spinach triangles and such like. The pie desserts should also be tried – peach and apricot, plum and apple or pecan nut, for instance.

The Anchor Inn keeps normal pub opening times and welcomes children, for whom there is a large paddock behind the building where they can play in safety. Telephone: 01420 23261.

- **HOW TO GET THERE:** Lower Froyle is 4 miles north-east of Alton and 6 miles south-west of Farnham. It stands just north of the A31 dual carriageway and can be reached from the Bentley turn-off.
- **PARKING:** There is a large car park in front of the pub and vehicles can also be left in various lay-bys along the village street.
- **LENGTH OF THE WALK:** 5 miles. Map OS Landranger 186 Aldershot and Guildford (inn GR 767438). The route to Bentley follows a clear, dry footpath and a village street. The return is by way of a quiet country lane and a splendid stretch of byway or 'green lane'.

THE WALK

Outside the Anchor Inn turn right to walk along the road under a line of pylons. A short way further on turn left along a private road, marked 'Coldrey'. A footpath pointer post shows that this is a public right of way, despite the fact that it runs in front of a line of private houses. These large, handsome buildings stand back from the gravel road.

The exact line of the Pilgrims' Way between Lower Froyle and Bentley can only be surmised. Most historians agree that it ran from

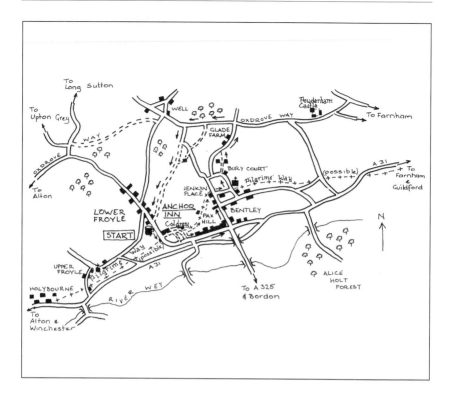

Coldrey to Bentley church, close to which stood a Holy Well. But whether the pilgrims headed straight for the church, over Pax Hill, or diverted to the centre of Bentley village, is not clear. Certainly the southern end of Bentley was a focal point for ancient packhorse routes and would have offered the pious travellers a suitable resting place.

Follow the gravel road to the farm buildings and then, where this turns right along a line of trees, continue straight on through a gate. A footpath arrow disc points down a wide grassy track. Soon you will see the fine Georgian façade of Coldrey House, over the wall on the left. The building actually dates back to before the 18th century and stands upon an even more ancient site. The grassy track joins the old tarmac drive and this you will follow as it bears right (*) to join the road into Bentley village.

(*Those who wish to walk directly to Bentley church, along the possible way of the pilgrims over Pax Hill, can go straight on across the fields. The signposted footpath leads across a valley with landscaped grounds (including a lake on the left) and then in sight of Pax Hill Nursing Home. It finally reaches the road at Jenkyn Place, at Bentley's northern end.)

A left turn at the bottom of the Coldrey House drive brings you soon into Bentley village, along the old A31 (now by-passed). Immediately before the junction, and next to the Memorial Hall, stands a wooden shelter enclosing a large map of the parish together with a brief history of the area. To reach the church turn left at the junction (up Hole Lane) and continue up the road along a raised footpath. Under a footbridge turn right opposite Jenkyn Place.

The return to Lower Froyle begins along the wide track that runs up beside the churchyard wall. Leaving the old Pilgrims' Way, walk northwards to reach the line of the prehistoric Oxdrove Way, which is about a mile distant. The route is clear enough. At Bury Court continue along a concrete drive (signposted as a footpath) which takes you across a little valley and up between a pair of brick-built cottages. Beyond these a footpath leads up the edge of a large field to a stile in the top corner. There, at the road, turn right to reach Glade Farm. Along this stretch be sure to turn around and look southwards for the views open out across the upper Wey valley to Alice Holt Forest. The Oxdrove Way is reached at the road junction above Glade Farm, where you turn left towards Well.

This road – in fact a quiet lane – runs along a wide ridge. There are views to the left and woodland on the right. Traffic has probably come this way for more than 2,000 years. It was a route still used in the Middle Ages and many Canterbury pilgrims would have chosen this road in preference to the alternative down in the valley.

In less than a mile from the Glade Farm junction you leave the Oxdrove Way, by turning left at the turning beyond the wood. This leads steeply downhill. Where this road bends left go straight on along a wide, tree-lined track marked as a 'Byway'. This 'green lane' leads directly back to Lower Froyle, where you turn left at the village pond to reach the Anchor Inn. But do not rush this stretch. It runs pleasantly up and down over the contours and offers views ahead. At one point a bench seat has been thoughtfully provided, to allow a more relaxed study of the panorama.

Pilgrims' Way

From Alton to Lower Froyle the Pilgrims' Way probably ran through the villages of Holybourne and Upper Froyle. From Bentley to Farnham it crossed the Wey valley at an angle. Many pilgrims would have aimed for Waverley Abbey, the first Cistercian monastery to be founded in England. Farnham itself was an important focal point for medieval drove roads, holding a large annual stocking market. The present A31 follows the line of an 18th-century turnpike road.

23

COMPTON
The Harrow Inn
≈❖≈

From Farnham to Guildford the Pilgrims' Way left the river Wey and climbed the narrow ridge of the North Downs. There was an old trackway along the chalk crest called the Hog's Back (turnpiked later and now the A31 trunk road) but the pilgrims preferred a more sheltered route. This ran below the windswept ridge along the green-sand, where there was a prehistoric way through the villages of Seale and Puttenham. The North Downs Way National Trail follows the same route but, where possible, avoids modern tarmac roads. This circular walk includes a 2½ mile stretch where the two Ways run together, east of Puttenham. The countryside is well wooded and two interesting villages are visited. One of these, Compton itself, contains the fascinating Watts Gallery.

Compton church, partly Saxon but mostly Norman, would certainly have been visited by the Canterbury-bound pilgrims. Unique in

England, it contains a two-storey chancel, the upper sanctuary of which probably once held sacred relics. Elsewhere in the village there are several fine timber-framed buildings, a couple of grand mansions and the Watts Mortuary Chapel. There are two pubs, the 16th-century Withies Inn at the southern end and the Harrow Inn, just south of the church.

The Harrow is neither very old nor very small but it still succeeds in being traditional and cosy. The three spacious bar rooms, on different levels, have low ceilings with beams, plain walls hung with old pictures and comfortable wooden furniture. Open fires burn in winter. Not surprisingly, the place is very popular.

The Harrow Inn serves a selection of real ales including Abbot, Greene King IPA and Hogs Back. The draught cider is Scrumpy Jack and there is a broad selection of wines. But it is the food offered that makes the place special. The range and quality are excellent and customers should build up a good appetite before arriving. There is a regular bar snacks menu book and a long list of daily specials on the blackboards, so the choice is wide. From soups, sandwiches, jacket potatoes and salads it rises through starters like grilled goat's cheese or avocado to main meals like Mediterranean fish casserole, lamb or pork grills with interesting sauces and game roasts. Vegetarians can have such dishes as stir-fry vegetables, pasta bakes and savoury pancakes. There are also traditional English puddings to enjoy, such as treacle tart and bread-and-butter pudding.

The Harrow opens all day Monday to Saturday and 9 am to 6 pm on Sunday. Telephone: 01483 810379.

- **HOW TO GET THERE:** Compton is 8 miles east of Farnham, 3 miles southwest of Guildford. It stands close to the A3 south of the junction with the A31. The B3000 runs through the village.
- **PARKING:** There is a pub car park and vehicles can also be left close by, in the lay-by in front of the village hall.
- **LENGTH OF THE WALK:** 5 miles. Map OS Landranger 186 Aldershot and Guildford (inn GR 956469). The footpath to Puttenham crosses a golf course. The rest of the circuit is along a clear, wide trackway well signposted.

THE WALK

Outside the Harrow Inn walk up the main road (B3000) to the church. Immediately beyond this turn left up Eastbury Lane, alongside the wall

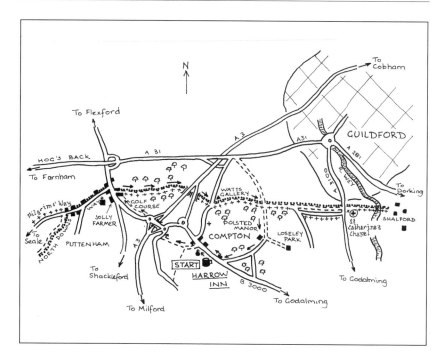

enclosing Eastbury Manor Nursing Home. This is marked as a private road and dead-end but a footpath signpost indicates it is a right of way for walkers. At the end of the tarmac follow the path that goes straight on beneath the trees and not the one that leads off left across the fields.

At the top of a short climb a stile leads to a path bearing right. This crosses a field, goes under a line of pylons and through a belt of young trees. More stiles bring you to the road where you turn right. Now cross the bridge over the A3 dual carriageway and follow the lane to Puttenham. Almost immediately, on the right next to Summer Wood, a footpath signpost points to a path between fences and hedges. This leads to the golf course.

Despite the many arrow discs showing the way, the footpath is not very clear. The fairways and golfers' tracks can mislead the walker. Keep straight on through a belt of trees and then aim for the cricket pitch. At the far side you walk through the golf club car park and emerge onto the road opposite the Jolly Farmer, at the eastern end of Puttenham village. The Pilgrims' Way and North Downs Way (together at this point) are joined here. Those wishing to visit Puttenham should afterwards return to the Jolly Farmer.

The Pilgrims' Way passes under the A3.

Puttenham is a pretty village with a mixture of old cottages, a Victorian-restored church with a 15th-century tower and a handsome Palladian-style priory. In the churchyard is an old well, rediscovered in 1972 when a yew tree fell down.

The wide sandy-gravel trackway, signposted as the North Downs Way, offers a very easy walk with no problems of route-finding. From opposite the Jolly Farmer it runs behind the clubhouse and through the golf course, with woodland upon either side. Beyond some handsome houses at Monksgrove you continue straight on at a staggered bridleway junction.

By this time you have left the golf course behind and a view begins to open up between the trees. In due course you walk under the A3. There are two bridges over the trackway, one carrying the dual carriageway, one carrying the old A3. Note the wooden crosses upon the latter bridge, designed by Sir Edwin Lutyens. These remind motorists that they are crossing the Pilgrims' Way.

The road at the northern end of Compton is soon reached. Turn right to visit the Watts Mortuary Chapel (and return to the village, if you wish to shorten the circular walk), turn left to visit the Watts Gallery (and to continue along the North Downs and Pilgrims' Way). The Chapel, built in 1896, is a curious Romanesque mausoleum with a carved frieze on the outside and wonderfully Art Nouveau murals inside. The Gallery displays many of the paintings, sculptures and sketches by the great Victorian artist, George Frederic Watts (1817-1904). He actually lived most of his adult life in Kensington but loved rural Surrey so much that he built a holiday home here at Compton. This was called Limerslease and the Gallery was sited close by. Today a tea shop helps entice visitors in but the works displayed persuade them to stay.

The North Downs (and Pilgrims') Way leads uphill from the Gallery entrance as a sandy trackway. Beyond some farm buildings it narrows, to climb more steeply through a wood. This is very pleasant, despite the busy A31 Hogs Back road being within earshot, up to the left. At the top of the ascent is a junction of paths, one corner of which is fenced off as the Loseley Estate Nature Reserve. For a distant glimpse of Loseley House itself you can continue straight on for ½ mile but the return to Compton begins from this junction.

Leaving the North Downs (and Pilgrims') Way turn right down the sunken track, under the trees. This brings you down to a country lane, next to Polsted Manor. Continue along this lane keeping straight on at the junction. This pleasant walk brings you to Compton village street, where you turn right for the Harrow Inn.

Pilgrims' Way/North Downs Way

From Farnham to Puttenham the Pilgrims' Way followed an old route through the villages of Runfold and Seale, now a quiet country lane. The North Downs Way runs parallel to this but slightly to the south, from Moor Park College on the river Wey to the wooded slopes beside Hampton Park. From the Loseley Estate to Guildford the two Ways run side by side down to the river Wey, crossing close to St Catherine's Chapel, Shalford.

CHILWORTH
The Percy Arms
❧

From Guildford to Gomshall the Pilgrims' Way climbed steeply out of the Wey valley to follow an old ridgeway track across St Martha's Hill, an ancient site of both heathen and Christian worship. Beyond this hill it continued along the Upper Greensand ridge, here a distinctive geological feature. The North Downs Way accompanies the Pilgrims' Way over St Martha's Hill but then climbs in order to follow the crest of the chalk North Downs escarpment. This circular walk includes a 2 mile stretch of the North Downs Way, to Newlands Corner, along which superb views can be enjoyed. The Pilgrims' Way is also followed, over St Martha's Hill on the outward journey and across pretty farmland on the return along the lower slopes.

Chilworth village itself is not especially old or beautiful but the little valley close by is fascinating. The waters of the Tilling Bourne were

29

used by the Chilworth Gunpowder Mills from the 17th century to the Great War, and at one time the area was so important that banknotes were also made here. Today the valley has been laid out as a country park with woodland paths, lake and riverside walks, preserved mill and foundry buildings, benches and information boards. The Percy Arms, at the eastern end of Chilworth and opposite the railway station, is said to be haunted by the ghost of a gunpowder mill worker. If it is, he is unlikely to recognise his surroundings.

The Percy Arms, although fairly old, has been totally modernised and refurbished. Many of the traditional features have been kept, like wooden floors and walls, beams and dado rails, open fires and old pictures, but the character is now light and airy, spacious and comfortable. Apart from a small bar room with dart board, there is one very large open-plan lounge on different levels, these enabling separate 'zones' to offer cosy corners. There is a conservatory and, outside, a beer garden with views towards the Downs. A function room operates upstairs and regular 'events' are held, like quiz nights.

From this Greene King house, IPA bitter is served together with Rayments and Abbot ales. The draught cider is Strongbow and the wines are mainly European. But it is the wide range and quality of the food offered that especially brings in the customers. A book menu lists the regular choice, and a blackboard lists the daily specials. Bar snacks include ploughman's lunches, salads, sausages and fish platters; main meals may include grills, steak and kidney pudding, chicken or beef in wine sauce, and salmon bakes. Vegetarians can choose bean burgers, nut cutlets or pasta dishes, and those with a sweet tooth can have such desserts as jam roly poly or chocolate fudge cake.

The Percy Arms keeps normal opening times and welcomes families. Telephone: 01483 561765.

- **HOW TO GET THERE:** Chilworth is 3 miles south-east of Guildford city centre, on the A248 road, which links Shalford to Albury. Dorking is 9 miles away eastwards.
- **PARKING:** There is a very large pub car park. Vehicles can also be left along the A248, which is fairly wide.
- **LENGTH OF THE WALK:** 5 miles. Map OS Landranger 186 Aldershot and Guildford (inn GR 031473). The route is very clear throughout, wide tracks being well signposted. The ground underfoot is generally dry but some steep gradients are involved.

THE WALK

Turn right outside the Percy Arms and walk westwards along the A248, towards the village centre. Before the level crossing turn right down Blacksmith Lane. This road leads across the valley of Tilling Bourne. Those with spare time should wander through the area of woods and lakes that you see on the right-hand side as you approach the river. Here were the old gunpowder mills. Those interested in nature and industrial archaeology could spend a happy hour or two exploring the site, perhaps with a picnic stop, for there are benches and seats thoughtfully provided.

Blacksmith Lane, which becomes Halfpenny Lane, actually leads all the way to the western side of St Martha's Hill, where the North Downs Way can be joined. Those not wishing to walk all the distance on tarmac can cut off a double bend by using a footpath. This is signposted left at the right-hand bend in the road, just beyond the river. An earthy path climbs alongside a hedge and then between fields. When Halfpenny Lane is rejoined continue left along it. A fairly steep climb, up through a cutting, will bring you to the North Downs Way. This crosses the road, coming in from the left next to a private camp site and going up to the right next to the 30 mph speed limit sign.

The wide, sandy bridleway, signposted as the North Downs Way, climbs up through a tree-scattered slope. The views begin to open out and soon you reach a wooden bar gate. Continue uphill. St Martha's Hill is now run as an open space by Surrey County Council, and many little pathways can be followed through the shrubbery. The North Downs Way and Pilgrims' Way run together up to the summit and down the other side. At the summit is the famous church of St Martha-on-the-Hill. Although largely rebuilt in Victorian times, this dates back to the 13th century. Historians say that it stands on a site sacred since the Bronze Age, when it was a hilltop centre for pagan worship, earthwork circles having been found close by. In medieval times the church was an important stopping point for the pilgrims, who gave offerings to help its upkeep.

The North Downs Way leaves the Pilgrims' Way on the eastern side of St Martha's Hill, immediately before an old wartime pillbox and a 'Downs Link' notice board. The wide sandy track that you have been following, marked by 'acorn' signs, joins a junction of paths at this point, under the trees. Turn left to follow a narrower track through the woods. The route to Newlands Corner is now clearly signposted. The North Downs Way should be followed all the way.

Descending to White Lane you continue along a woodland path that

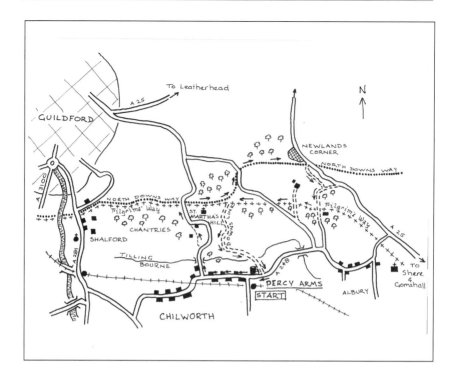

runs alongside the road, on the left, and then, crossing over that road, you fork right at the first junction. Emerging onto an open grassy hillside with fine views to the right, you contour beside a woodland edge, at the top of the scarp slope. Round the bend on the far side is Newlands Corner where a large car park, refreshment kiosk and toilets give comfort to foot and car travellers alike.

Leaving the North Downs Way, the way back begins along a clear gravel byway. This is marked by a red arrow, close to the North Downs Way finger post, next to the A25 (which you do not cross). After descending at an angle down the slope this byway turns sharp right to continue southwards as a sunken track between hedged banks. After bearing left this old way (called Water Lane on maps) meets the line of the Pilgrims' Way, which crosses east-west. Some cottages stand high above the byway on the left. Turn right here, up an earthy track that climbs and curves below the trees.

The Pilgrims' Way is now followed for about a mile. The path is deeply rutted but generally firm, dry and sandy. From the woodland bear right to cross a field at an angle and then, over a farm track,

St Martha's Hill from Newlands Corner.

continue westwards alongside another woodland. Between some paddocks, you soon reach the road. Cross over and walk through the woods opposite. You are now re-entering the St Martha's Hill open space. Joining a wide sandy trackway, continue westwards along the line of some log posts. These lead you to the wartime pillbox and bridleway junction seen earlier.

The Downs Link begins here, as indicated by the notice board. This 30 mile long route was established in 1984 to link the North and South Downs, joining the latter at Steyning. This is the route to follow back to Chilworth. The wide, sandy trackway runs south, descending slowly down to the Tilling valley. The views are wonderful, ahead to the Weald, over Albury to the left. After a right, then a left bend the Downs Link becomes a firm farm track. This crosses the Tilling Bourne and joins the A248. Turn right for the short walk back to the Percy Arms.

Pilgrims' Way/North Downs Way

From Guildford to St Martha's Hill, the Pilgrims' Way and North Downs Way run together as a clear bridleway alongside Chantries wood. East of Newlands Corner the North Downs Way keeps to the higher ground, following woodland paths, whilst the Pilgrims' Way, further south, winds past Albury church to Shere and Gomshall.

WESTCOTT
The Crown Inn

From Gomshall to Dorking the Pilgrims' Way followed the edge of the North Downs but there is doubt about its exact route. Some historians say that it climbed the chalk downs and then ran along the crest of the ridge, corresponding with the present course of the North Downs Way. Other historians maintain that it kept to the greensand, along the terraced slope, above and parallel to the present line of the Guildford to Dorking railway. Both theories could be correct, different tracks being used during the five centuries or so in which pilgrims travelled this way. The circular walk includes a 1½ mile stretch of the North Downs Way from White Downs to Ranmore Common. This is mostly a woodland walk but there are still wonderful views to be enjoyed towards the Sussex Weald.

Westcott is surprisingly quiet considering its close proximity to Dorking. It is also a very attractive village with a good scattering of old buildings and a triangular green boasting a thatched bus shelter and dovecot. The large Victorian church stands on the slope above the High Street. A mile westwards is Wotton House, now a college, the one-time home of diarist John Evelyn (1620–1706). There are three pubs in Westcott, all of which can be recommended: the Cricketers, the Prince of Wales and the Crown Inn. The last named stands at the eastern end, on the south side of the main road.

This is a small, cosy establishment with an old-fashioned atmosphere and a friendly, unpretentious welcome. The public bar has a pool table, the two-roomed lounge is decorated with saddles, harnesses and other horseriding equipment. Open fires burn in winter and customers can sit outside in a raised beer garden in summer.

The Crown serves no fewer than four cask ales, which is unusual in Surrey. These include Adnams Broadside and Charles Wells Bombardier. There is also a full range of other drinks: draught cider, stouts and wines. The choice of food is excellent, from simple bar snacks to full meals and daily specials, all of which are homemade. Local game is available in winter and spit roasts are a regular option. The 'butchers sausages and real chips' is always popular. Vegetarians are catered for and there is a wide choice of desserts.

The Crown Inn keeps normal pub opening times and families are welcome. Telephone: 01306 885414.

- **HOW TO GET THERE:** Westcott is 2 miles west of Dorking, on the A25 road to Guildford. Junction 9 (Leatherhead) on the M25 is 7 miles away to the north.
- **PARKING:** There is a pub car park. Vehicles can also be left along the side streets of the village, but preferably not along the busy A25.
- **LENGTH OF THE WALK:** 5 miles. Map OS Landranger 187 Dorking and Reigate (inn GR 144486). Clear trackways and footpaths are used throughout but the route does include some stiles and steep gradients. Signposts are frequent.

THE WALK

From the Crown Inn walk westwards along the A25, through the village and past the turning that leads up to the church. Beyond the houses and Rookery Drive (which is on the left) turn right along Balchins Lane. After about 200 yards turn left up a tarmac track signposted as a bridleway. The open countryside now beckons and the scarp slope of the North Downs rises up from the distant fields to the right.

Beyond the woodland ignore the right turn to Stockman's Coomb

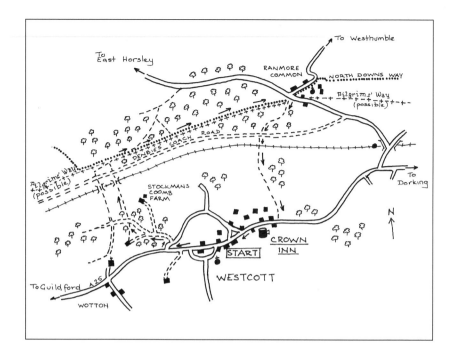

Farm and continue to the fork 100 yards further on. Bear right here along a rough track that climbs slightly towards another woodland. At the far edge of this woodland, as the track bears left, you should notice a footpath cutting across. Follow this to the right as it runs beneath the trees to a plank bridge over a ditch. The hills should now be straight ahead, across the fields. The route is clear, to the top of White Downs.

The footpath continues along the edges of three large fields, crosses a brick bridge over the railway line and climbs the edge of another field to a stile. Beyond this a wide track runs along the foot of the slope. Ignore this and continue steeply uphill through the shrubland. Be sure to look back when you stop for a breather – the view towards Leith Hill is lovely. Towards the top, close to the edge of woodland, you join a wider chalky track that comes up from the left. This you follow up to the right, to a farm gate. A blue arrow disc and acorn sign show that you have met the North Downs Way.

Incidentally, the trackway that runs along the foot of the scarp slope, which you crossed, is known as Denbies Coach Road. This was once the approach road to Denbies, a 19th century house (now demolished) on Ranmore Common. This road probably follows the line of an ancient track. Some say this was the original route used by the Canterbury pilgrims. Perhaps it was. Certainly this way would have been well sheltered from the north winds during winter months.

The route to Ranmore Common is very clear and needs little description. About 200 yards beyond the farm gate the trackway forks. To the left a bridleway is marked by a blue arrow disc, to the right a narrower footpath is marked by a yellow arrow disc. Follow the latter. This path contours around Pickett's Hole, a wooded coombe, and widens on the far side as another bridleway joins from the left. Thereafter the wide earthy pathway is almost dead straight, as it contours along the top of the slope.

Ignoring all other paths going down or up on either side, continue all the way to the far end of the woodland, where a right fork takes you to a stile and gate. On the way the view opens out to the south, across Westcott towards the Weald. Beyond the stile and gate is Steer's Field (National Trust) which you cross to reach Ranmore Common, the church spire being clearly visible ahead.

The way back to Westcott begins opposite the lane that leads to the church. Go through a kissing gate by a North Downs Way signpost, alongside a garden hedge, but then, instead of turning right (as if to retrace your steps to White Downs) go straight on. Beside a wire fence walk steeply downhill to a kissing gate in the bottom corner. Now a clear footpath leads down through woodland. Across a wide track (Denbies Coach Road again) and down a flight of rough steps you descend to the farmland below. By field edges and stiles you cross the railway line (beware trains!), walk beside a wood and follow a wide grassy track across the valley. The last stretch runs up behind some back gardens to the A25 road. There you turn right for the Crown Inn.

Pilgrims' Way/North Downs Way

From Gomshall to White Downs the Pilgrims' Way is not clearly defined. It probably climbed at an angle to reach the dry chalk slopes below Hackhurst Downs. The North Downs Way is further north, meandering through the forest of Netley Heath. East of Ranmore Common the Pilgrims' Way (again lost) probably skirted the spur of the Downs, whilst the North Downs Way now takes a more northerly route, over the top of the hills. The two Ways come together at the crossing of the river Mole, north of Dorking.

BETCHWORTH
The Arkle Manor
❧❀❧

From Dorking to Reigate the Pilgrims' Way skirted the southern slopes of Box Hill before climbing up around Pebble Coombe to continue along the crest of the chalk escarpment. The North Downs Way, however, keeps to the top of the hills almost all the way, by a more circuitous route. Where possible the pilgrims followed ancient trackways along the 'spring line' at the base of the scarp slope. Only where this slope proved too steep for traversing did they climb to the ridge. This circular walk includes a 2 mile stretch of the North Downs Way from Box Hill to Betchworth Quarry. Part of the return route follows the Pilgrims' Way along a terraced track. The views to be enjoyed are spectacular throughout, and the many areas of woodland offer beauty and interest all year round.

Betchworth is a lovely old village, stretching down from the quarry-scarred hills to the river Mole. The landscaped grounds of Broome Park lie to the east and the elegant Betchworth House (17th century) stands at the southern end. Close to the latter is the church, which dates back to Saxon times, an ancient barn and a picture-postcard little street. There are two pubs in the village, the Red Lion and the Dolphin. These serve good food and real ales and are deservedly popular.

The Arkle Manor, west of the village on the main road towards Dorking, is a large 'Harvester' establishment. It therefore specialises in food rather than real ales and caters for groups and families rather than devoted beer drinkers. A full range of drinks is, of course, offered (like Bass ales, Harveys' stouts, Blackthorn cider and various table wines) but it is the menu selection that draws in the customers. Everything is well cooked and reasonably priced. From the bar snack menu there are jacket potatoes, burgers, granary sandwiches and 'basket' meals; from the full restaurant menu there are spit roasts, grills, salads and various fish dishes. Vegetarians can choose such items as spiced beanburgers and vegetable crumble; those with a sweet tooth can have all manner of ices, cakes, tarts and crumbles.

Though modern, the decor has a pleasant Edwardian atmosphere with a wooden bar counter and brass fittings, settle seats, a beam-and-plank ceiling and wallpapered walls with old pictures. The large brick fireplace is decorated with golfing mementoes. There are two large open-plan lounges, a separate restaurant and a beer garden at the back.

Normal pub opening times are kept except at weekends and on bank holidays when you can be served all day. Telephone: 01737 842110.

- **HOW TO GET THERE:** Betchworth is 3 miles east of Dorking and 3 miles west of Reigate. The village stands to the south of the A25.
- **PARKING:** There is a very large pub car park. Vehicles can be left in the village but this is a mile away.
- **LENGTH OF THE WALK:** 6 miles. Map OS Landranger 187 Dorking and Reigate (inn GR 199505). The route is very easy to follow but there are some steep gradients.

THE WALK

Almost opposite the back of the Arkle Manor, across the lane, a footpath signpost points south, down a track called Mill Hill Lane. This is the route to Brockham. Follow it all the way ignoring other turnings and crossing Kiln Lane, until you reach a junction of paths. Here, turn right down a trackway that dips and curves below the trees and crosses a bridge over the river Mole. Bearing right thereafter you soon reach the

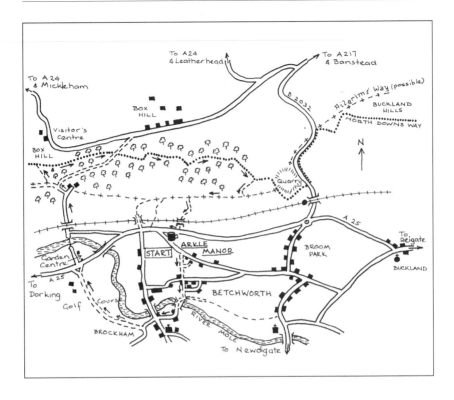

Duke's Head and Brockham village green. Those with time should stay awhile for this is a very attractive spot, with old buildings all around and a handsome church. The green, which is very large, was once used regularly as a cricket pitch and W.G. Grace is said to have played here.

Keeping the green to your left continue across the main village street, past the old pump and down Old School Lane. This descends to cross a tributary of the river Mole. Immediately after the bridge turn right along a wide gravel track, signposted as a bridleway. Beyond some houses this track narrows slightly and becomes more earthy but the route is very clear. The North Downs are ahead, about a mile away. Continue straight on, through the golf course and (keeping well to the right of the club house car park) across the A25. Walk down the gravel lane past Dorking Garden Centre, over the metal footbridge across the river Mole and then up the road ahead that runs under the railway bridge. You are now beginning the long climb up Box Hill.

Immediately after passing under the line of pylons bear left up a wide gravel path marked by an arrow disc. This, incidentally, is part of the

Box Hill.

Pilgrims' Way (but at this stage in our walk we do not stay on it for long). Soon you reach a fork where stands a National Trust Box Hill sign. Do not bear right here, up a deeply rutted path that climbs beneath the trees. Instead keep left, to a gate and stile. Beyond these bear right up a grassy/earthy path (leaving the Pilgrims' Way to contour at a lower level). A steep climb, at an angle up the North Downs scarp slope, brings you to the crest along which runs the North Downs Way. Here you turn to the right.

The summit of Box Hill is very soon reached and the constant flow of visitors to this spot attests to its popularity. The view is glorious and a panorama platform helps the identification of distant points of interest. The North Downs Way continues past the Ordnance Survey 'trig point' and into the woods where yew, juniper and, of course, box trees grow. The visitors' centre is just out of sight up to the left.

Ideally, the North Downs Way would have contoured along the crest of the hills all the way to Betchworth Quarry. Sadly, suitable rights of access could not be negotiated and so a more circuitous, up-and-down route was determined. Regular arrow disc marker posts help guide the walker through the sloping woodlands.

41

At first the North Downs Way does contour, forming a slightly winding track, at one point crossing a gulley via wooden steps. Soon, however, a sharp left turn takes you up a long flight of steps. Further on another flight of steps lead down the slope, these being followed by a steep pathway climb up. Immediately beyond a curious memorial stone to 'Quick, An English Thoroughbred', yet another flight of steps lead you down again. At the bottom of this particular descent, beyond an old overgrown quarry, you leave the North Downs Way for the journey back to the Arkle Manor.

A wooden post with arrow discs marks the point of return. To the left the North Downs Way continues, to curve around the still active Betchworth Quarry. To the right an earthy path descends under the trees. Follow the latter direction. After a right, then a left bend you reach a wider path that runs along the bottom of the scarp slope. This is the Pilgrims' Way and you turn right to follow it, alongside a wire fence. After about 300 yards turn left, downhill away from the woodland. Follow the footpath that runs across a field (beside a phantom hedgerow), under a line of pylons and then, half right, to the far corner. Continue under the railway bridge to the main road, where you turn right for the short walk back to the pub.

Pilgrims' Way/North Downs Way

From Dorking to Box Hill the Pilgrims' Way, having crossed the river Mole at Burford, contoured the lower scarp slope. It cannot now be followed easily, parts of it having disappeared, other parts running across private land. The North Downs Way, however, climbs directly and steeply up to the Box Hill summit. East of Betchworth Quarry, from Pebble Coombe, the Pilgrims' Way ran over the Buckland Hills but, once again, its exact route cannot easily be walked. The North Downs Way runs along the base of the Buckland Hills before regaining height at Juniper Hill, whence it continues along the crest to Reigate Hill.

MERSTHAM
The Railway Arms
❧

*F*rom *Reigate to Oxted the Pilgrims' Way continued along the crest of the North Downs. This was probably the easiest route since the scarp slope along here is especially steep, and the numerous spurs and coombes made a hillside trackway impracticable. The North Downs Way now takes a similar route, diverting here and there to avoid such obstacles as roads, quarries and private land. This circular walk includes a 2 mile length of the North Downs Way from Ockley Hill to White Hill, a stretch probably walked by the pilgrims. Despite the closeness of the M25 motorway the countryside hereabouts is very pleasant and the views extend across the Weald to the South Downs.*

Merstham was famous in the Middle Ages for its sandstone quarries, the stone from which was used at Windsor Castle, old St Paul's Cathedral and the original London Bridge. Today the village has been urbanised, as a suburb of Redhill. However, the 13th-century church and Quality Street, a pretty 17th-century assemblage, help recall Merstham's past.

The Railway Arms, on the main road round the corner from Quality Street and almost opposite the large and popular Feathers Inn, is a small unpretentious pub. Notwithstanding its name, the building dates back to the 17th century and despite some structural changes made in Victorian times many original features survive. Inside there are two small rooms, a public bar with dart board and a cosy lounge which doubles as a dining area. There are low ceiling beams, wood panelled walls hung with pictures and horse brasses, and traditional furniture.

This is a Marston house serving Marston's Pedigree and Banks real ales, Dry Blackthorn cider and a small selection of wines. The range of food on offer is also fairly limited. Bar snacks include soups, jacket potatoes, ploughman's lunches and salads; main meals tend to be simple dishes like casseroles, lasagne, sausages and chips and, for vegetarians, cauliflower cheese. A small choice of daily specials is also written up on a blackboard. But the lack of menu diversity is more than compensated by the quality of the cooking, the helpings and the reasonable prices. Indeed, for a friendly welcome, wholesome food and a cosy, convivial atmosphere the Railway Arms is hard to beat.

Normal pub opening times are kept; children are welcome and a rear patio garden offers a popular sitting area in summer. Telephone: 01737 642289.

- **HOW TO GET THERE:** Merstham is 2 miles north of Redhill and 2 miles east of Junction 8 (Reigate) on the M25. It stands on the A23.
- **PARKING:** There is a pub car park. Vehicles can also be left in many of the side streets, including Quality Street, where space permits.
- **LENGTH OF THE WALK:** 6 miles. Map OS Landranger 187 Dorking and Reigate (inn GR 290535). This is the very easy walk in terms both of route-finding and terrain. Clear paths and country lanes are used. Some slopes are encountered but none should cause difficulty.

THE WALK

The North Downs Way actually runs through Merstham, along Quality Street. This takes its name from J.M. Barrie's famous play. The two leading actors in its original production, Seymour Hicks and his wife Ellaline Teriss, once lived at Old Forge at the end of the street. From the Railway Arms turn right and then right again along Quality Street, past a collection of attractive and old buildings.

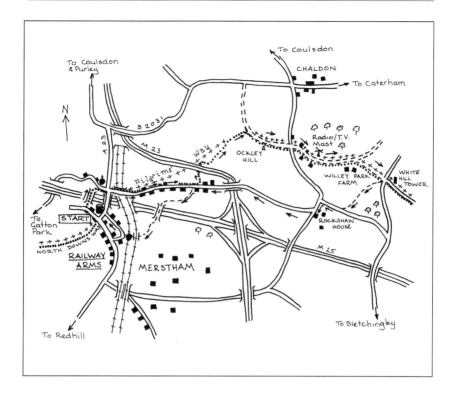

The North Downs Way crosses the M25 by a footbridge and turns right alongside the churchyard. Those with spare time should look in the church, a fine 13th-century building containing some interesting stained glass windows. Outside, the lych gate has been made from oak beams and stone from an old mill that once stood nearby.

Across the A23 the North Downs Way continues along Rockshaw Road for about ½ mile. There is a pavement all the way and you can admire some of the detached residences that you pass. In due course take the path signposted to the left, immediately before a bungalow. The route runs under the M23 and, bearing right, makes the long ascent up the scarp slope of the Downs. The noise of the motorway still intrudes but the view opens out behind, in compensation. Through a belt of trees halfway, you continue at an angle to the top where you meet a wide track. Turn right along this, past the OS trig point. A signpost points the way. The view south is now wonderful, across to the Weald. Gatwick Airport can hardly spoil the sweep of the distant horizon.

This handsome lodge stands at the entrance to Rockshaw House.

The route of the North Downs Way, as it runs eastwards for a mile along the crest of the hills, needs little detailed description. It is a clear, well-signposted track all the way. Cross over the road and continue between the large detached houses to Willey Park Farm, passing a radio/TV mast on your way. Thereafter, beyond an old stone dovecot, bear right to follow a rough tarmac farm lane all the way to Stanstead Road, at the top of White Hill.

The return to Merstham begins immediately before this road but you should look, first, at White Hill Tower, behind the trees opposite. This is a curious edifice, a derelict folly. It was built in 1862 by a certain Jerimiah Long. From the top it would be possible, on a clear day, to see northwards across London.

The return is very easy and fairly direct. Leaving the North Downs Way, follow the bridleway running west between fences and towards the vale below. In due course this track bears left and descends more steeply through woodlands. At the bottom turn right along the road to the next junction. There turn left, then right to follow the lane signposted to Merstham. This is the end of Rockshaw Road and the handsome lodge to Rockshaw House stands opposite.

Having crossed over the M23 and passed the North Downs Way signpost on the right (followed earlier), turn left through a kissing gate. This footpath runs down between gardens, bears right to cross the M25 by a footbridge and then descends via a long flight of steps to pass under a railway line. Across the station platforms you can follow Station Road back to Merstham High Street.

Pilgrims' Way/North Downs Way

From Reigate to Merstham the Pilgrims' Way and North Downs Way run together through Nut Wood and around Gatton Park – unfortunately very close to the M25 motorway. Gatton Park, originally landscaped by 'Capability' Brown, contains a curious collection of Classical buildings. It is now occupied by a children's home. From White Hill to Oxted the two Ways run together, or parallel, over Gravelly Hill and Tandridge Hill. Once again, the M25 is very close all the way.

WESTERHAM
The George and Dragon
❦

*F*rom Oxted to Sevenoaks the Pilgrims' Way descended to follow the
bottom of the scarp slope once again. As the line of the North Downs
ridge straightened so the pilgrims took a low, direct route to the old
churches at Titsey and Chevening. The greensand rock underneath
this area made the ground here almost as dry as the chalk uplands, so
the medieval travellers were given easy passage even in winter
months. The North Downs Way keeps to a level higher up the
escarpment, following an irregular course along tracks and
footpaths. This circular walk includes a 2 mile stretch of the North
Downs Way, from Betsom's Hill to Hogtrough Hill, and (upon the
return) follows a short length of the Pilgrims' Way. The M25
motorway is close by but this detracts little from the enjoyment of the
views and diverse wildlife.

Westerham boasts some famous connections. General James Wolfe lived here as a boy (at Quebec House, now National Trust owned) and Sir Winston Churchill lived at nearby Chartwell for his last 40 years. The 13th-century church has a stained-glass Wolfe memorial window by Edward Burne-Jones, and Squerryes Court, close by, houses a notable museum and art gallery. This is an old, handsome little town.

There are many good pubs here. The George and Dragon is especially popular for it is a friendly place with an old-fashioned atmosphere. It is said that General Wolfe stayed here immediately before his departure for Canada, where he was killed at the Battle of Quebec (1759).

Inside there is one large open-plan bar room with a lounge at one side, behind a wooden screen, and a separate restaurant in front. There are beamed ceilings, panelled walls hung with tankards and old pictures, creaky floorboards and open fireplaces. In summer, tables are set out in front of the pub.

In recent years the George and Dragon has been extensively refurbished to expand its service and facilities. It is now open all day (thus offering morning coffee) and boasts a carvery restaurant which operates to customer acclaim. Functions are catered for, by arrangement. There is a wide choice in both food and drink: everything from sandwiches, salads and pastas to full roasts and daily specials, washed down with a selection of real ales (John Smith and Courage Directors for instance), draught ciders and wines. Special diets should not be a problem and groups can be accommodated, on request. There are also frequent 'theme evenings' which should not be missed.

Normal opening times are kept in winter but all day opening is more common in summer. Telephone: 01959 563071.

- **HOW TO GET THERE:** Westerham is 4 miles east of Oxted and 5 miles west of Sevenoaks. It stands at the junction of the A233 (from Biggin Hill) and the A25.
- **PARKING:** There is a pub car park but vehicles can also be left along nearby sidestreets. Parking around Westerham green is restricted.
- **LENGTH OF THE WALK:** 5½ miles. Map OS Landranger 187 Dorking and 188 Maidstone (inn GR 446541). The route is well signposted but some steep slopes are encountered.

THE WALK

Turn right outside the George and Dragon and right again down the B2024 signposted to Croydon. This leads you through the outskirts of Westerham and under the M25. About 500 yards beyond the motorway

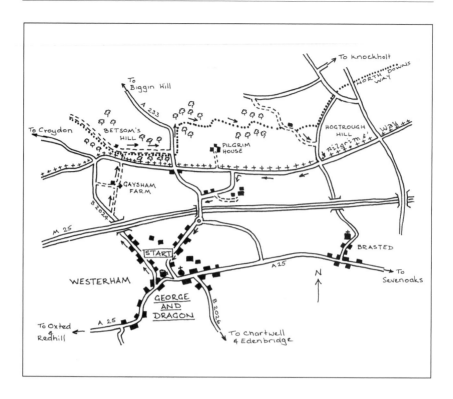

turn right up a wide farm track signposted as a footpath. The Downs are now ahead with Betsom's Hill on the skyline. At Gaysham Farm continue across the farmyard and curve round behind the barns to the track on the far side. This leads you, in the same direction as before, directly to the foot of the scarp slope. Cross over the road (which, incidentally, follows the line of the Pilgrims' Way) and climb uphill along a narrow path which runs between gardens and under the trees. Very soon you reach a wide gravel track that runs along the slope. This is the North Downs Way and you turn right along it.

For reasons of landownership the North Downs Way, from the west, has descended to the lower slopes of Betsom's Hill. From here eastwards it continues as a well-used drive, serving a number of large residences which are hidden up amongst the trees. Southwards there are occasional glimpses of the view over Westerham. The National Trail regains its route along the crest of the hills on the other side of the A233. After crossing that road to a stile, therefore, you turn left and begin the ascent.

For the next mile or so the route is somewhat circuitous as the North Downs Way gains height. The path is well worn and well signposted so there should be little difficulty in finding the direction. After climbing along the edge of a large field you enter a woodland. After a while the path contours, at first under the trees and then along the bottom edge of the wood. After a left turn you climb steeply. After two flights of rough steps and a stile you continue uphill along a field edge. Beyond another stile (from where you can look round at the view) you climb further through more woodland. The crest is soon reached where you turn right along a clear gravel track.

After the next gateway you continue along the top of a grassy slope, below which is the farmstead called Pilgrim House. The view beyond, across the vale, is worth a moment's stop. After the next gate and stile, and through a belt of woodland, you continue up to the left along a field edge. At the top corner bear right along the top edge of the same field to the far corner. There a couple of stiles lead you through to the next field where you continue in the same direction. The hedgerow is still on your left, but not for long. Soon you cross a stile in that hedgerow and continue in the same direction along a wide trackway. There is now a large private garden, complete with tennis court, to your left. It is not far before this track bends right and the North Downs Way is signposted to the left along a narrower track.

The return to Westerham begins here as you keep right and leave the North Downs Way. Follow the trackway as it descends, bears left and eventually joins the road that runs down Hogtrough Hill. Turn right down that road to the junction at the bottom. Turn right again and follow the lane which is now called, appropriately, 'Pilgrims' Way'. After less than a mile turn left down a narrower lane which takes you, in a curve past a farm, to the A233 at the northern edge of Westerham. Turn left to cross the M25 back to the George and Dragon.

Pilgrims' Way/North Downs Way

From Oxted to Betsom's Hill the Pilgrims' Way has, for the most part, been lost. The Titsey estate is private and cannot be walked across. The North Downs Way contours along the scarp slope of the Downs but climbs in order to skirt Titsey at a higher level through the Titsey Plantation. East of Hogtrough Hill the Pilgrims' Way continues for a while as a modern road but is lost again at Chevening. The North Downs Way, further north, maintains its route along the top of the hills, passing close to Knockholt village.

KEMSING

The Wheatsheaf

ᵉ⬥ᵉ

From Sevenoaks to Wrotham the Pilgrims' Way crossed the river Darent at Otford (where stood the Archbishop's palace) and continued eastwards along the scarp slope. The pilgrims deliberately kept to a height above the narrow clay vale which, in medieval times, was prone to flooding. The North Downs Way accompanies the Pilgrims' Way across the Darent valley but then climbs to follow, once again, the crest of the hills. This circular walk includes a 2 mile stretch of the North Downs Way on the outward route, and a 1½ mile stretch of the Pilgrims' Way on the return. Thus, both upland and lowland walking can be enjoyed. There are wide views across open Kent countryside, and attractive hamlets.

Kemsing was a stopping point for medieval pilgrims and remains a popular tourist centre. On the small village green is St Edith's Well, named after the daughter of the Saxon King Edgar. She was born at Kemsing in AD 961 and the spring here was thought to possess healing qualities. The nearby church (restored in Victorian times) dates back to the Normans and contains some ancient stained glass, delicate carving and a magnificent altar canopy.

At the village centre are two excellent pubs, the Bell Inn and the Wheatsheaf. The former dates from the 18th century and is said to occupy the site of an old monastery. The latter is more recent, but still very traditional in both atmosphere and decor. In terms of hospitality and range of food and drink there is little to choose between them. Perhaps you should sample both!

The Wheatsheaf, a Courage house, especially concentrates upon its food, which is well prepared and reasonably priced. Bar snacks include such items as burgers, jacket potatoes, salads, sandwiches and sausages; main meals include various roasts, grills and pies as well as curries and chilli con carne. Vegetarians can have veggi-burgers or pasta bakes; big eaters can finish with a caramel and apple pie, or liqueur mousse. Daily specials are also written up on blackboards. For drink, Courage Best ale, Scrumpy Jack cider and many different wines are offered.

There is one main bar room/lounge plus a smaller room with pool table and darts. There are beamed ceilings and walls, wooden furniture, old pictures hung up and a brick fireplace. All is cosy and friendly. Normal pub opening times apply weekdays but all-day opening operates at weekends. Telephone: 01732 761038.

- **HOW TO GET THERE:** Kemsing is 3 miles north-east of Sevenoaks, 2 miles east of Otford. It can be reached from the A25 at Seal or from the A225 at Otford.
- **PARKING:** There is a pub car park but the large free public car park immediately beside the Wheatsheaf may prove more convenient.
- **LENGTH OF THE WALK:** 5 miles. Map OS Landranger 188 Maidstone (inn GR 556587). The route is well signposted but the circuitous nature of the North Downs Way here requires care in navigation. Some steep slopes are encountered.

THE WALK

Turn right outside the Wheatsheaf and right again opposite St Edith's Well up a signposted footpath which runs between the houses and alongside the public car park. At the top end cross over the road and go through two kissing gates. Now the steep climb begins. The grassy

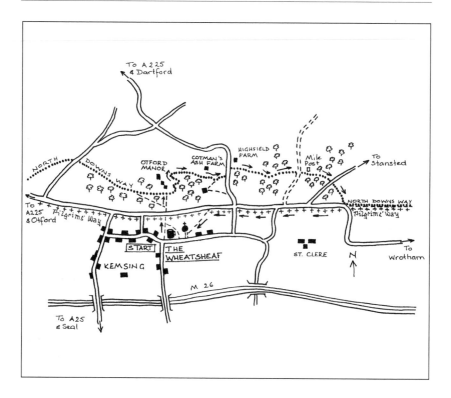

hillside is now run by Kemsing Parish Council as an open amenity space and seats have been placed here and there for the convenience of visitors. It is a popular spot on warm summer evenings.

Ignoring the kissing gate and path on the left, halfway up and close to woodland, climb to the skyline where a large wooden cross has been erected. In front of this runs a wire boundary fence. This marks the edge of the Otford Manor estate, now run by a Christian organisation.

The North Downs Way runs alongside the wire boundary fence here so you turn right to follow it. Shortly a kissing gate leads you through into the estate. Walkers should keep strictly to the route indicated by the frequent arrow discs since this is private land. Continue uphill and straight on until the ground levels off. Before a farm gate turn right and go over a stile to follow the edge of a wood, which is to your right. Round the corner of the field another stile leads you back onto an earthy path. Across more stiles this path crosses and then runs beside a wide trackway. At the end of this you leave the Otford Manor estate and meet open farmland.

From now on the North Downs Way becomes less complicated as it runs eastwards along the crest of the hills. Between the trees to the right are regular views so this stretch should not be rushed. Continuing along the edge of a large field and crossing a stile in the far corner, you reach a clear wide earthy path under the trees. Beyond another stile you enter another large field. For about 100 yards keep close to the hedgerow on your right. Then, over a stile in that hedgerow continue in the same direction down a track all the way to a road. There turn left, uphill.

The North Downs Way continues a short distance up, opposite Cotman's Ash Farm and immediately before Highfield Farm. It is signposted. Along the edge of a barnyard and down a rutted track you soon reach a stile. Beyond this continue across a pasture field towards distant woodland, tall wooden stakes marking the route. After following the edge of the next field you reach that woodland. The path winds through it clearly. On the far side of the wood, after crossing a track, you should notice a North Downs Way mile post. Farnham is 60 miles away, Canterbury is 54 miles and Dover 65 miles. From this spot the view is, once again, spectacular.

At the edge of the next wood take the left fork, walk past an old dew pond (flint-lined and of unknown antiquity) and follow the field edge eastwards. A gate in the far corner leads to a path running through the woods of the St Clere estate. In spring the bluebells here are wonderful. Soon you descend to a road. The North Downs Way now turns south to go down the scarp slope. From the road, 20 yards below the point where you joined it, a footpath signpost points the way. By some rough steps and a steep descent across two fields you reach the bottom, at a road junction. Turn right.

The route back is along the Pilgrims' Way, now a country lane. Ignoring other turnings go straight on all the way, past St Clere House, to the outskirts of Kemsing. There you can cut across the large playing fields directly to the church. The Wheatsheaf stands beyond.

Pilgrims' Way/North Downs Way

From Sevenoaks to Otford the exact line of the Pilgrims' Way, across the Darent valley, is lost. East of Otford, however, it is followed by a modern lane almost all the way to Wrotham. The North Downs Way keeps to the crest of the hills where possible. It descends at St Clere, from where it accompanies the Pilgrims' Way along the base of the scarp slope.

BIRLING

The Nevill Bull

❦

*F*rom *Wrotham to the river Medway the Pilgrims' Way continued along the scarp slope before striking downhill, away from the chalk ridge. The Medway valley was a great obstacle in medieval times, with its meandering waterways and mudflats, and the route of the old road is not known for sure. Historians think it probably crossed the river at Snodland where a greensand outcrop allowed a slightly drier passage. The North Downs Way continues along the chalk hills, to cross the Medway near Rochester beside the M2 motorway. This circular walk includes a 1½ mile stretch where the North Downs Way and Pilgrims' Way run together, contouring along the dry chalkland slope. An impressive Neolithic burial site (Coldrum Stones) is passed on the route.*

Birling, Ryarsh and Addington are three small villages, almost joining together, sited upon the fertile lowlands below the North Downs. They are pretty and surprisingly quiet considering their close proximity to the industrial areas along the river Medway. Birling is the smallest of the three.

The Nevill Bull, located at the central road junction, takes its name from the coat of arms of the one-time local landowning family. Owned by the Laurel Pub chain it serves a range of real ales (eg Abbots, Flowers), draught ciders and wines. But it is the food served which brings in the customers. There is something for everyone, portions are generous and the quality of the cooking reaches the highest levels. Bar snacks include sandwiches, jacket potatoes, salads and sausages; main meals include grills, roasts and casseroles; vegetarian items include cream and broccoli bake and vegetable lasagne. Daily specials are written up on the blackboard and these could be lamb and apricot pie, kiev and stroganoff (various types). There is also a separate restaurant.

Inside there is a large open-plan bar room with timber features everywhere – beams, posts, screens. The walls are bare brick and the fireplace bare stone. Pictures and brassware decorate the walls. All is very traditional and comfortable.

Normal pub opening times are kept and families are welcome. Telephone: 01732 843193.

- **HOW TO GET THERE:** Birling is 5 miles east of Wrotham and just 2 miles west of the river Medway at New Hythe. It is close to Junction 4 of the M20 motorway. It can be reached from the A20 at Addington or from the A228 at Snodland.
- **PARKING:** There is a large car park. There are few parking spaces elsewhere in the village.
- **LENGTH OF THE WALK:** 5½ miles. Map OS Landranger 188 Maidstone (inn GR 680605). The route is very clear throughout as well-worn paths and tracks are used. There are no steep slopes to negotiate, since the scarp slope of the North Downs is not climbed.

THE WALK

From the Nevill Bull walk westwards along the road to Ryarsh. Birling and Ryarsh are almost joined and there is a pavement all the way. Ignoring, if you can, the M20 to the left you can admire the view to the right, where the steep slope of the Downs rises to a wooded summit. Past the Ryarsh village hall and opposite the Duke of Wellington pub, turn right up Chapel Street. Follow this all the way as it curves left and

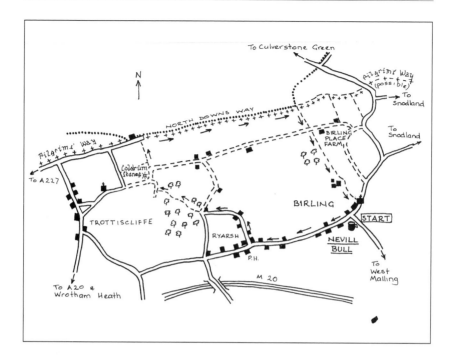

leaves the village behind. At the T junction with Workhouse Road/Park Farm Road you will see a stile almost opposite. Take the path beyond.

The Coldrum Stones are less than a mile away and are soon reached. Over a number of stiles the path runs beneath the trees, then along the woodland edge and across a clearing. Through another patch of woodland it continues across a field and joins a track coming in from the left. Bearing right here you soon meet a concrete drive, along which about 100 yards further on stands the archeaological site now owned by the National Trust. Standing upon a knoll the Stones – actually a long barrow – are an impressive sight. Four monoliths stand in a half-circle and a raised tomb forms an apex on one side.

The North Downs Way runs along the base of the scarp slope 500 yards away. A path leads directly there, alongside some field edges. A large house stands close to the point where you join it.

Turning right you reach the end of a tarmac lane, from where a wide earthy path continues eastward. The North Downs Way and Pilgrims' Way are coincidental along this stretch and the route provides a lovely, easy walk. There are trees either side and the path keeps to the same height as it contours along the base of the scarp slope. Ignoring

The Coldrum Stones passed on the route.

other tracks, on left and right, you continue for more than a mile. At one point, where a track goes downhill back to the right, the North Downs Way kinks before re-establishing its eastward direction. In due course you reach a junction. The North Downs Way arrow points up to the left across a stile, the Pilgrims' Way path continues straight on and another path goes right, down across the fields. Follow the latter.

The way back is very direct. The path is almost dead straight and, for much of the distance, Birling church can be seen ahead. You walk along the edge of one large field, cross a farm lane and continue along a grassy track between hedges. Across a shallow valley and beside a wood you then skirt to the left of a farmstead and, over a couple of stiles, eventually reach the church. From the church it is only a few yards back to the Nevill Bull.

Pilgrims' Way/North Downs Way

From Wrotham to Birling the Pilgrims' Way and North Downs Way run together, except for the section behind Trottiscliffe where the latter climbs to the crest of the hills. East of Birling the exact line of the Pilgrims' Way is lost whilst the North Downs Way keeps to the hills behind Upper Halling and Cuxton, mostly through woodland.

BLUE BELL HILL
The Upper Bell Inn

From the river Medway to Maidstone the Pilgrims' Way, having regained firm ground, continued along the spring line at the base of the chalk escarpment. There is a legend that it crossed the Medway valley beside a prehistoric avenue of stones linking two Neolithic burial sites, but nothing remains of any such causeway. The burial sites do survive, however: the Coldrum stones (seen on walk 11) and Kit's Coty (seen on this walk). The North Downs Way, upon leaving the M2 bridge, maintains its route along the top of the chalk ridge. This circular walk follows the North Downs Way for 2 miles, as far as Boxley, and returns along the Pilgrims' Way.

Blue Bell Hill village actually forms the southernmost suburb of Chatham. It is dominated by the M2/A229 interchange. However, there are excellent views from here and a picnic site has been laid out upon the crest of the hills.

The Upper Bell Inn stands on the other side of the bridge from the picnic site, over the A229. It is a very popular place with tourists, villagers and local office workers, and deservedly so. It is friendly, cosy and welcoming. The place has been refurbished in recent years but the old-world charm survives: the large open-plan bar room is heavily timbered with ceiling beams, posts and panelled walls decorated with old pictures. A new restaurant is proving very busy, whilst outside, beside the beer garden, is a children's play area.

Owned by the Laurel Pub chain, the Upper Bell serves real ales (eg Flowers and London Pride) and a good selection of stouts, ciders and wines. Food ranges from ploughman's lunches, 'doorstep' sandwiches and burgers to salads, curries, pastas, pies and roasts. Vegetarians will find many options too and the daily specials are very popular. This establishment opens all day from late morning onwards. Telephone: 01634 861149.

- **HOW TO GET THERE:** Blue Bell Hill is 4 miles north of Maidstone and 5 miles south of Rochester. It stands on the hills overlooking the Medway valley and the A229 runs in a cutting immediately below. Junction 3 on the M2 motorway is close by.
- **PARKING:** There is a very large car park behind the pub, from which entrance is gained into the bar room. The picnic area on the other side of the A229 bridge also has a large car park.
- **LENGTH OF THE WALK:** 5½ miles. Map OS Landranger 188 Maidstone (inn GR 747621). The route is well signposted throughout and the footpaths used are all well worn. There are some steep gradients and care should be taken after wet weather.

THE WALK

Walk up Mill Lane, which runs alongside the Upper Bell, to the far end. Where it turns sharp right to become Warren Road (which follows the line of the old Roman road to Maidstone) go straight on, across a stile. The footpath you want is not the one half-left across a field but the one that follows a wire fence along into the woods. In springtime the bluebells are lovely here and the noise of the nearby motorway fails to spoil such a pretty sight. This hill is well named.

The route to the North Downs Way is very easy to follow. Across some stiles you continue along the winding path as it runs parallel to the

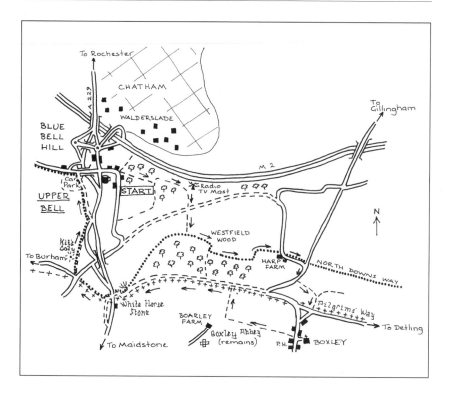

M2, ignoring a path to the right. Beyond the trees you proceed along a field edge to a radio station where you turn right alongside the perimeter fence. Down the tarmac drive you meet a road. Cross straight over to follow a footpath which cuts across a field to a distant wood. This is Westfield Wood and the North Downs Way is joined at the point where you reach the trees.

Turning left you follow the National Trail along the edge of Westfield Wood, keeping the field to your left. Soon after passing under the line of pylons turn right, down a track into the woods and then, almost immediately, left uphill again. Arrow discs show the way. (Those wishing to shorten their circular walk, omitting Boxley, can leave the North Downs Way here and continue steeply downhill, at the bottom turning right along the Pilgrims' Way.)

The North Downs Way now runs as a fairly straight woodland track along the top of the scarp slope. To the right, through the trees, is the occasional glimpse of a view, to the left are the open hilltop farmlands. In due course, however, the scenery changes. The North Downs Way turns sharp left to climb from the edge of the wood and alongside a wire fence. It then turns right to reach Harp Farm. Beyond Harp Farm you join a road and continue straight on (round a bend) to meet a junction. Here you leave the North Downs Way by turning right.

The way back to the Upper Bell begins with a steep descent into Boxley. About 300 yards from the junction, and just before the gradient steepens, turn left down a signposted bridleway. This goes down through a wood, bearing right on its way to the bottom. At the road cross straight over and take Styles Lane towards the village centre, turning left at the next junction.

To reach the Pilgrims' Way, avoiding a road walk, take the footpath which begins alongside the King's Arms. From the edge of the village this goes straight across two large fields and then sharp right to reach the foot of the scarp slope. Turn left along the Pilgrims' Way - here a wide gravel track - to return to Blue Bell Hill. This is a pleasant stretch, through woodland for most of the way. The White Horse Stone will be seen on the right, shortly before the A229. This is a sarsen megalith, possibly marking a prehistoric burial site.

Having passed under the A229, beside a petrol station, you continue along a signposted byway which looks more like a footpath. The Pilgrims' Way and North Downs Way, for this short stretch, are running together. At the road junction, however, they divide again. From here you follow the North Downs Way all the way back to the Blue Bell Hill picnic site, at first along a steeply ascending woodland track and then along Old Chatham Road, beside the modern dual carriageway.

On the way be sure to notice Kit's Coty 300 yards up from the road junction. This is a Neolithic dolmen in fine condition. The three upright and one 'table' stones are still in place, forming one of the best preserved burial chambers in southern England.

From the picnic site it is only a short walk over the bridge to the Upper Bell.

Pilgrims' Way/North Downs Way

The pilgrims are likely to have crossed the Medway by a ferry that linked the ancient churches at Snodland and Burham Court, which still stand on the riverbanks. The exact line of the Pilgrims' Way, however, is now lost until it reaches Kit's Coty. From there, eastwards, it ran through Boxley and Detling, along a line now mostly occupied by country lanes. The North Downs Way follows the hilltop from the M2 bridge, running high above Wouldham and Burham.

HOLLINGBOURNE
The Windmill

From Maidstone to Lenham the Pilgrims' Way continued to contour along the bottom of the scarp slope, keeping above the damper ground of the vale below. The North Downs Way follows the crest of the hills as far as Hollingbourne where it descends. Thereafter it accompanies the pilgrim route. This circular walk includes a 2½ mile stretch to Harrietsham where the two Ways run together. The return is along another ancient trackway. The countryside is very pretty and some old, attractive buildings can be admired.

Hollingbourne nestles prettily under the chalk escarpment. The Tudor manor house was once the home of the Culpeper family and is said to be haunted by Catherine Howard (fifth wife of Henry VIII), whose mother was a Culpeper. The church is worth a visit for its numerous memorials, ornate chapels and - to be viewed only by application to the vicar - some wondrous altar cloths.

The Windmill, which is situated at the Eyhorne Street end of Hollingbourne, close to the A20 and M20, is a pub not to be missed. Offering an excellent range of food and drink in a wonderfully traditional setting, it is cosy, welcoming and friendly. Inside there is a large open-plan bar room arranged in three semi-separate areas. On one side is an intimate 'sitting room' with armchairs and bookshelf, on another side, behind a large brick inglenook fireplace, is the dining area. Everywhere there are low ceiling beams, wood panelled walls and old furniture, including cupboards and dressers. Plates, old kitchen tools, bottles and brassware are hung up. Outside at the back is a sheltered garden with a pergola – ideal for summer evenings.

This Laurel Pub chain inn sells a range of real ales (like Boddingtons, Flowers, Fremlins and Brakspear), Strongbow draught cider and over twelve types of wine. The food is excellent, the regular choice being supplemented by daily specials, listed around the food hatch. There are salads, sandwiches, ploughman's lunches, roasts, fish dishes, casseroles and grills. Old faithfuls like bangers and mash, liver and onions and steak and kidney pie compete with more luxurious meals like cannelloni Provençal, vegetable korma and Stilton mushrooms. Desserts include ice cream sundae, chocolate fudge cake and apple pie.

The Windmill is open all day. Telephone: 01622 880280.

- **HOW TO GET THERE:** Hollingbourne is 5 miles east of Maidstone, very close to Junction 8 on the M20 motorway. Leeds Castle is nearby. The village stands on the B2163.
- **PARKING:** There is a large pub car park at the rear. Vehicles can be left elsewhere, provided no obstruction is caused.
- **LENGTH OF THE WALK:** 6 miles. Map OS Landranger 188 Maidstone and 189 Ashford (inn GR 833545). This is a very easy, fairly level walk along clear wide trackways. Those with time may like to explore the village of Harrietsham.

THE WALK

Turn right outside the Windmill and walk up the main village street, which is the B2163. Shortly after the railway bridge, as the road bends right, follow the footpath that is signposted between the war memorial and the school, both on the left. A rough tarmac path takes you directly to Hollingbourne church. Beyond this continue along the B2163, past the Elizabethan manor house that once belonged to the Culpepers, to the northern end of the village. Here you will see a further selection of

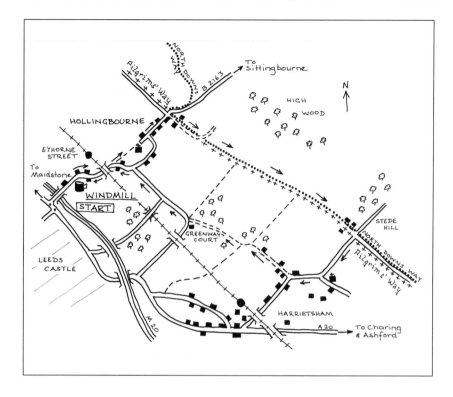

old and interesting buildings including an old village forge, a malthouse and the Dirty Habit pub. Turn right at the last named, which was once called the 'Pilgrims' Rest' since it stands on the Pilgrims' Way.

The North Downs Way and Pilgrims' Way run together here and the route is extremely clear. At first it is a tarmac lane, past a few houses, but it soon becomes a gravel, then a grassy, track. In due course, where the firmer surfaced section bends left to serve a local farm, it is signposted as a 'Byway'. This should be followed all the way to Harrietsham, in an almost straight line. Ignore all other tracks and paths on either side.

It is a lovely walk that should not be rushed. Running along between fields, it follows the base of the North Downs scarp slope. To the left are the well-timbered hillsides, to the right are views across the Vale of Kent towards the Weald. Along one section the track climbs a little, then descends as it crosses a downland spur but, that apart, the route is level. After about 2 miles you reach Stede Hill. The track ascends as it becomes a rough tarmac service lane for some houses and meets a road.

Here you leave the North Downs Way by turning right and walking downhill to Harrietsham church.

This is an interesting church and should be explored by those with spare time. It is mainly 15th-century but does contain parts of an earlier, possibly Saxon, building. Inside are some fine tombs (including that of Sir William Stede) and an unusual Norman font. The oldest part of Harrietsham village lies ½ mile away, beyond the railway line.

The return to Hollingbourne is along an ancient route called The Greenway, which runs parallel to the Pilgrims' Way/North Downs Way but further downhill. It is now used mostly by local farm traffic but in medieval times it was the main route linking the two villages and used by drovers and market traders.

From Harrietsham church the road bends right, then left. At the second bend go straight on along a tarmac lane past some houses. This is a bridleway, despite also being labelled as a 'Private Road'. The route is very clear. Beyond the farm buildings the track becomes a wide earth-and-grass way running between fields and along a line of trees. After a left-then-right kink it continues in the same direction, at first narrower than before (alongside a wire fence) and later a bit wider again. It winds a little, and is joined by other paths and tracks, but the route is obvious. Beyond Greenway Court it becomes a tarmac lane. Continue straight on to the road at Hollingbourne where you turn left to reach the Windmill.

Pilgrims' Way/North Downs Way

From Maidstone eastwards the pilgrims used an existing trackway that linked the churches of Boxley, Detling, Thurnham and Hollingbourne, such places offering the travellers rest and refreshment stops. The North Downs Way runs along the hill crest above these villages, giving modern walkers a route with wide views. Eastwards from Harrietsham the two routes run together to Lenham and beyond.

CHARING

The Queen's Head

❧❦❧

From Lenham to Wye the Pilgrims' Way and North Downs Way run together along the scarp slope of the chalk hills, just above the spring line. Wye, on the Great Stour river whose valley cuts through the Downs, was an important medieval town. Pilgrims gathered here, those from Winchester meeting those from Europe who had travelled up from the Channel coast. Today Wye is also the place where the North Downs Way splits, at the western end of the 'Canterbury' or 'Kent Loop'. On the hillside above the town one arm of the National Trail turns north to Canterbury, the other arm continues east, to cross the Stour valley and heads for the coast. This circular walk follows a 2½ mile length of the Pilgrims' Way/North Downs Way, as far as Westwell. The countryside all around is beautiful, with woodlands, meadows and open chalk downland.

Charing must have been a busy place in the Middle Ages. There was a magnificent archbishop's palace here, where both Henry VII and Henry VIII were entertained, and the church contained the block upon which John the Baptist was beheaded, a relic captured by Richard the Lionheart. Apart from the 14th-century gatehouse little remains of the palace today and the block disappeared at the Reformation. Still, Charing is a pretty place and well worth investigating, especially for its plethora of ancient cottages.

At the bottom of the High Street, on the corner of the A20, stands the Queen's Head. This is not an especially old building but it is still an attractive, traditional-style pub. Inside there is a large open-plan bar room in three sections, with a back room set aside for a pool table, reached through a small dining area. There is much timber-work, with ceiling beams, wall posts and a plate rack around the frieze. Old pictures and brassware are hung around and the furniture (like the settle seating) is old-fashioned. In all, a most pleasant and cosy atmosphere.

This is a freehouse serving various real ales (like Wadworth 6X, Flowers IPA and Brakspear), draught cider (Scrumpy Jack) and a good selection of wines. Large blackboards list the daily food choices. These may include such bar snacks as baguettes, sandwiches, jacket potatoes and salads, and such main meals as steak and kidney pie, lasagne, cod and chips and – for vegetarians – omelettes or pasta bakes. Traditional desserts include spotted dick and treacle pudding.

The Queen's Head is open all day, from late morning, and welcomes children. Telephone: 01233 712253.

- **HOW TO GET THERE:** Charing is 6 miles north-west of Ashford, close to the junction of the A20 and A252 roads. It can easily be reached from Junction 9 of the M20.
- **PARKING:** There is a pub car park and vehicles can be left, also, in some of the local back streets.
- **LENGTH OF THE WALK:** 6 miles. Map OS Landranger 189 Ashford (inn GR 953493). This is an extremely easy walk along a clear trackway on the outward journey and, mostly, quiet country lanes upon the return. There are no steep slopes to negotiate.

THE WALK

From the Queen's Head walk up the High Street, through the centre of the village. The Royal Oak Inn will be seen on your left, the lane leading

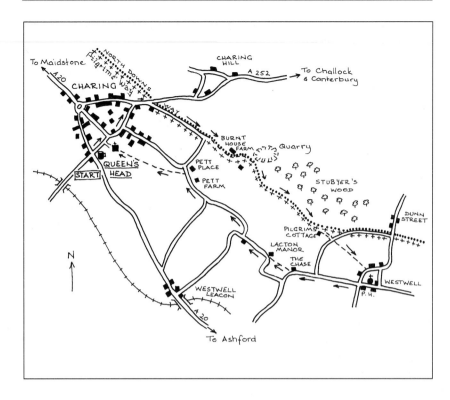

to the church on your right and, further up still, the King's Head pub on your left. There are many other interesting buildings to admire, and a few shops should you require any walking or picnic supplies. At the top of the village, at the A252, turn right. After about 400 yards turn right again, down a tarmac lane. This is actually called 'Pilgrims Way' and is signposted as the North Downs Way.

The route is very clear and straight all the way to Westwell and should not need any detailed description. Beyond the last houses of Charing the tarmac lane becomes a gravel track. Go straight on at the first junction and then, almost immediately after Burnt House Farm, follow a left-then-right kink as the track avoids Burnt House Cottage.

Here the route is signposted as a 'Byway'. It climbs a little and passes the entrance to a quarry. Thereafter it provides a lovely walk contouring along the North Downs scarp slope. To the right are views towards the Kent Weald – a beautiful prospect, notwithstanding the M20. Up to the left is Stubyer's Wood, the track following the bottom edge of its trees. In due course, just past Pilgrims Cottage, the track forks. Leave the

North Downs Way at this point by taking the right-hand route, which leads down to the road.

To reach the hamlet of Westwell cross directly over the road and follow the footpath opposite. This crosses a large field diagonally downhill. In the far corner the path winds through a thick hedgerow to emerge onto the road. Turn right to reach the junction where stands the Wheel Inn. Those with time and interest should look at the church (left at the junction) before starting their return to Charing (right at the junction). It has a nave of columns, round and octagonal, a stone-vaulted chancel and a triple sedilia. Much of the building is Early English in style, dating from the 13th century.

The way back is almost entirely along country lanes. There is very little traffic and the walk is very pleasant. There are also some fine buildings to appreciate. One short stretch, from a house called The Chase to Lacton Manor, can be done alternatively by footpath but this does not really shorten the distance. At the first road junction go straight on, at each of the next three junctions keep right.

Of particular note architecturally are Pett Farm and Pett Place, the latter being a magnificent 18th-century mansion with 19th-century Dutch gables. These houses will be reached almost at the eastern outskirts of Charing. From here a footpath can be followed to Charing church. This will be seen on the left where the road bends right. It crosses some fields and runs through a belt of trees to reach a playing field. Beyond this is the churchyard, a short walk from the Queen's Head.

Pilgrims' Way/North Downs Way

From Lenham to the hills above Westwell the Pilgrims' Way and North Downs Way co-exist, along a route probably used since prehistoric times. East of Westwell, however, the two routes diverge. The exact route of the Pilgrims' Way is not known, as it winds through the area now called Eastwell Park. It possibly kept to the uplands to skirt Boughton Lees and Boughton Aluph. Many pilgrims, of course, would have travelled into Wye for a night's rest. The North Downs Way splits at Boughton Lees. The northern arm runs through Boughton Aluph, the eastern arm runs through Wye.

CHALLOCK
The Chequers
ᴇᴥ❖ᴥᴐ

From Wye to Chilham the Pilgrims' Way kept to the western side of the Great Stour valley, climbing the chalk slope at an angle to the top of Soakham Downs. From there it continued along the crest of the hills, here forming a spur. The North Downs Way splits near Boughton Lees and its northern arm follows the same course as the Pilgrims' Way over Soakham Downs. This circular walk includes a 2 mile stretch where the two Ways run together along the top of the chalk ridge. There are views across the Great Stour valley to be enjoyed but essentially this is a walk through Forestry Commission woodland.

Challock is not a big village in population, but it does cover a fairly large area. Around an expansive village green stand a number of grand houses, many with well maintained shrub-filled gardens. There is a pleasant mixture of architectural styles and ages, and a scattering of handsome trees. The church is a mile away to the south, in Eastwell

Park, an area landscaped in the 18th century.

The Chequers faces the village green and has long been popular with both locals and ramblers. Dating back to the 17th century, it is wonderfully unmodernised. Inside all is dark, cosy and traditional. There are low ceilings with beams, wooden parquet floors and plain walls of bare brick or plaster. A large inglenook fireplace contains a woodburning stove and all around are old pictures and brassware. The old furniture includes comfortable armchairs and there is even a well-stocked bookshelf in one corner. The many bar rooms are all small, including the dining area, this adding to the general atmosphere of friendliness and welcome.

This is a freehouse serving Master Brew and Harveys real ales, Strongbow and Theobolds draught cider and a good selection of, mainly, European wines. A large range of home-made food is also offered from snacks and salads to copious main meals. Steaks, scampi, chicken, steak and kidney pie and 'foreign' dishes like lasagne, curry or chilli con carne are all regularly cooked, together with specials for vegetarians such as vegetable cannelloni.

Normal pub opening times are kept and families are welcome. Telephone: 01233 740672.

- **HOW TO GET THERE:** Challock is 11 miles south-west of Canterbury and 6 miles north of Ashford. It stands on the junction of the A252 and A251 roads.
- **PARKING:** There is a pub car park and vehicles can also be left along the nearby lanes which are quiet and uncluttered.
- **LENGTH OF THE WALK:** 6½ miles, or 4 miles if walkers park their cars at the King's Wood Forestry Commission Car Park and Picnic Site. Map OS Landranger 189 Ashford (inn GR 009505). All the paths and trackways in this forest are well marked and well used so there should be few difficulties.

THE WALK

Those not starting at the King's Wood Forestry Commission car park should turn left outside the Chequers (along Blind Lane), right along the footpath that crosses the cricket pitch and then right again down the A251, where a grass verge is provided for much of the distance. The car park will be reached a short way down the lane signposted to Wye. This is a popular spot with both locals and tourists. Various forest trails have been laid out and interesting wooden sculptures act as picnic furniture. Any number of walks can be planned and families could spend many happy hours here.

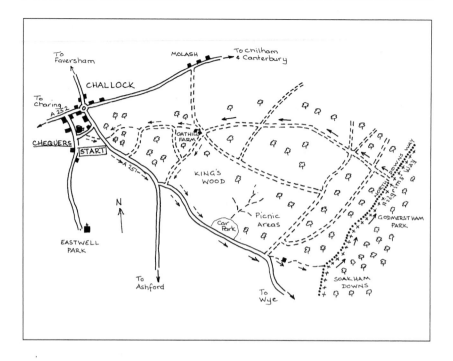

To reach the North Downs Way, where it crosses Soakham Downs, walkers should follow the road in the Wye direction for about 500 yards. Another smaller parking area will be reached on the left. From here take the gravel-grass track signposted as a footpath and not the wide sandy track beyond a bar gate. The route required is a farm road that runs beside a garden fence.

Through a farm gate continue alongside a wire fence, which is to the right. Ignoring a stile in this fence keep straight on, towards the distant view. After the next gate the path continues along the top of a field and then, at an angle, towards woodland on the far side. The gate and stile at the edge of that woodland lead back into Forestry Commission woodland. The wide trackway ahead is soon joined by the North Downs Way, which comes in from the right. Continue straight on.

The National Trail is very clear along this stretch, being a wide earthy-stoney trackway well marked with arrow discs. Keep to the left at the first fork, go straight on at the junction of paths and keep left at the next fork. The North Downs Way ascends slightly and then levels off, to give a lovely forest walk. There are occasional views to the right – for the track is fairly high up on this chalk upland – but the woods dominate the scenery. Many of the trees here have been coppiced, since this is a well-managed forest, so the undergrowth is full of wildlife and interest. After about 2 miles you reach a point where a grassy track leads off to the left. Nearby stands a North Downs Way milestone: Farnham is 103 miles away, Canterbury is 10 miles and Dover 28 miles. From this point the return to Challock begins.

Follow the grassy track, left, as it descends to a wide gravel trackway running along a shallow valley. Cross this and continue up the wide track opposite. This curves through the woods, dips and climbs and is joined by other smaller paths. In due course a wide grassy track joins from the right and then, after a short ascent, a junction of tracks is reached. Continue straight on along a red sandy trackway. This takes a long left-handed curve to Oathill Farm Riding Centre, which will be seen on the right beyond a farm gate.

Those who began the walk at the King's Wood Car Park should ignore the gate to Oathill Farm and continue along the sandy trackway. This leads to the lane where a left turn will bring you to the car park. Those walking to the Chequers pub should go through the gate and follow the path that runs alongside the edge of the farm buildings. Beyond these a woodland path leads on to a main sandy track. This should be followed to a point where it bears left, when you take the footpath that goes half-right. This crosses a clearing, runs through a belt of trees and alongside a woodland. Challock will soon be reached, across the fields and beyond the cricket pitch.

Pilgrims' Way/North Downs Way

The Pilgrims' Way, now lost through Eastwell Park, probably climbed Soakham Downs and then aimed directly for Chilham. Private landownership means it cannot be followed into Chilham. The North Downs Way joins the Pilgrims' Way on Soakham Downs but leaves it on the slopes above Godmersham Park. From there it follows a lower, more circuitous, route into Chilham village.

CHARTHAM
The Artichoke Inn
❧

From Chilham to Canterbury the Pilgrims' Way completed its journey from Winchester along the western slopes of the Great Stour valley. Although its exact route has been disputed by historians, it is agreed that it climbed to the chalk ridge above Chartham and then cut through the Iron Age hillfort of Bigbury Camp. The North Downs Way now takes the same route but, where possible, keeps away from modern roads. This circular walk includes a 2 mile stretch where the North Downs Way and assumed route of the Pilgrims' Way run either together or parallel. There are woodlands, orchards and views to be enjoyed as well as the lakes and meadows beside the Great Stour river.

Chartham is an attractive place. The handsome Gothic church overlooks a large village green and dotted all about are ancient buildings, ranging from picturesque cottages to grand timber-framed and Classical residences.

The Artichoke Inn must be one of the oldest of the buildings, reputedly dating back to the 14th century. It stands round the corner from the Chartham Paper Mill. Inside there are two main bar rooms – a restaurant and lounge – and a plethora of traditional features like ceiling beams, timber framing, bare brick walls and a central fireplace where an open log fire burns in winter months. Old pictures decorate the walls and a collection of jugs hang from the ceiling.

This is a Shepherd Neame establishment serving Master Brew and Canterbury Jack real ales, Dry Blackthorn cider and a good selection of wines including some English country (fruit) wines. The bar snack choice is especially good, the list being written up on a large blackboard. There are sandwiches (normal and toasted), salads and omelettes all with a range of fillings. Cheeseburgers, ploughman's lunches, cottage pie and lasagne may also figure in the menu. As far as main meals are concerned the choice is bigger – the landlord boasting 12 starters and 15 main courses in the à la carte selection. For vegetarians these are such dishes as vegetable creole and avocado/Camembert parcels.

Normal pub opening times are kept and children are welcome. Telephone: 01227 738316.

- **HOW TO GET THERE:** Chartham is just 3 miles south-west of Canterbury, close to the A28 (Ashford) road. The junction with the A2 dual carriageway is only 2 miles away.
- **PARKING:** There is a pub car park across the road from the main entrance. Vehicles can also be left here and there around the village, along the side streets.
- **LENGTH OF THE WALK:** 5 miles. Map OS Landranger 179 Canterbury (inn GR 108548). The route is very easy to follow since it uses country lanes and clear trackways throughout.

THE WALK

Turn left outside the Artichoke Inn and walk through the village, past the church and over the level crossing. Cross over the main A28 and continue uphill on the far side, along the lane signposted to Chartham Hatch. With increasing height, the countryside begins to open out, especially to the left where orchards and woodlands cover the rolling downland slopes. After another railway level crossing you climb to a road junction close to a telecommunications mast. On the left is Hoppers Oast, an old oasthouse tastefully converted into apartments. At

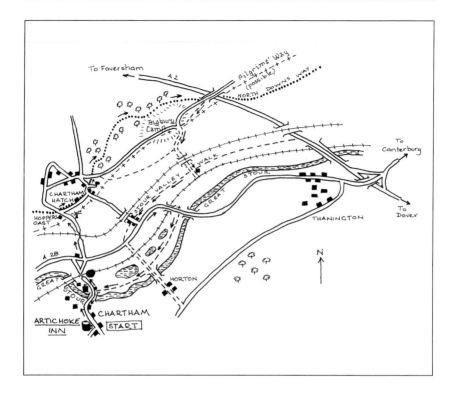

this point the North Downs Way comes in from the left and continues along the lane to the right. Turn right to follow it.

● The North Downs Way accompanies New Town Street into Chartham Hatch, past orchards and the Chapter Arms, a pub with a good reputation and a large garden. Go straight on at the next junction, but only for about 100 yards. Where the road bends left and Nightingale Close begins on the right, continue down the pathway ahead, between garden fences. This is signposted as the North Downs Way. Indeed, from this point there are regular signposts and arrow discs so the route should be clear.

Cross over the next road and follow the path along the right-hand edge of the playing field. Beyond this continue down a wide track that leads through a wood, alongside an attractive orchard (which now has 'access land' status) and, bearing left, back into woodland. Now follow the main track as it curves between the trees. Despite the ever-increasing noise of the nearby A2 dual carriageway this is a lovely stretch, with occasional views to the left across orchards and hop fields.

Many of the trees either side have been coppiced, to encourage new branch growth from the base.

Soon you will notice that the land on the right rises, since the track actually skirts the northern slopes of Bigbury Camp. This is thought to have been constructed by the Celts, in the century before Christ, and used in the fighting against both the Belgae tribes, from Northern France, and the Romans. Today paths wander around the shrubby hilltop, giving access to those wanting a closer look. At the north-eastern corner of Bigbury Camp the North Downs Way meets the road which takes it over the A2. You leave the National Trail here.

The return to Chartham begins at the stile almost opposite. A footpath leads diagonally beside an orchard, southwards to a lane. Turn left and follow this lane downhill. It runs between orchards, bears right, bends left and goes under the railway. About 500 yards further on, close to a farm, turn right along a clear grassy track. This is signposted as the Stour Valley Walk, an officially designated route from Lenham to the coast via Ashford and Canterbury. It will lead you all the way back to the Artichoke, through orchards and meadows.

The first mile is a fairly straight track across a large area given over to apple trees, with views down to the river and old gravel pits, now forming attractive lakes. The second mile, having turned left at the lane and crossed the A28, is a riverside pathway beside fields and willow trees. A splendid end to a lovely walk.

Pilgrims' Way/North Downs Way

From Chilham the pilgrims probably travelled via Shalmsford Street before making the long climb over Bigbury Camp, but the exact route they took is not known for sure. From Bigbury they descended directly to Canterbury Cathedral, where Thomas à Becket's shrine awaited. The North Downs Way takes a more northern route, through Old Wives Lees to Chartham Hatch.

KINGSTON
The Black Robin
❧❀❧

From Canterbury to Woolage the North Downs Way, now running alone, crosses the rolling chalk uplands which form the 'dip' slope of the North Downs escarpment. To the north the countryside dips gently down towards the Thames estuary. This circular walk includes a 2 mile stretch of the North Downs Way as it climbs Barham Downs. The scenery all around is beautiful and there are three lovely villages to explore, for those with time to spare.

Kingston is a pleasant little village nestling in the valley of the Nail Bourne. The old church is surrounded by groups of houses and tall trees, the whole making an attractive ensemble. The Black Robin stands at the eastern end, almost surrounded by rolling fields.

This is a freehouse famous not so much for its range of drinks as for its menus. The food is excellent: fresh seasonal dishes are changed daily and the variety is adventurously biased towards the unusual. Customers, not surprisingly, come from far afield to enjoy the meals on offer. Together with your real ale (Master Brew), draught cider (Scrumpy Jack) or well-chosen Australian or Chilean house wine you could choose a simple snack such as a Highwayman's Roll. But you should, perhaps, treat yourself to one of the tempting items listed on the blackboard. This could be smoked venison, haggis with mustard sauce, Thai-style beef stir-fry or veal and mushrooms in cream sauce. There are always meals suitable for vegetarians – avocado baked in tomato and garlic, for instance.

The building dates back to the 18th century and the name is derived from a local highwayman, who terrorised northern Kent at that time. There are two main bar rooms, the smaller acting as a public bar, the larger as a lounge-cum-dining room. There are ceiling beams, bare brick walls and a great deal of wood panelling. The floors are bare tile and wood and the large brick fireplaces are well used in winter months. The furniture is especially old and curious, consisting of a mixed selection of settles, pew chairs and rough kitchen tables. Children are welcome and normal pub opening times are kept from Wednesday to Sunday. The Black Robin is closed on Mondays and Tuesdays but walkers have two pubs to choose from in nearby Barham. Telephone: 01227 830173.

- **HOW TO GET THERE:** Kingston is 5 miles south-east of Canterbury, very close to the busy A2. It is 10 miles north of Folkestone.
- **PARKING:** There is a large pub car park. Elsewhere in the village vehicle space is limited.
- **LENGTH OF THE WALK:** 4 miles. Map OS Landranger 179 Canterbury (inn GR 201513). Country lanes, clear trackways and well-marked footpaths are used so route finding should be easy. The A2 is crossed twice so care should be taken at these points.

THE WALK

Outside the Black Robin turn left and walk northwards along the lane that follows the valley, not eastwards along the narrower lane that ascends directly to the A2. The point where you need to cross the dual carriageway is ½ mile away. This is reached by going up the bridleway that you meet at the second bend in the road. A signpost points the way. Cross straight over the A2 and continue up the lane opposite. This climbs steadily, offering a view behind across the Nail Bourne valley. After about 400 yards the North Downs Way is reached, crossing from left to right. Turn right to follow it, an arrow disc showing the direction.

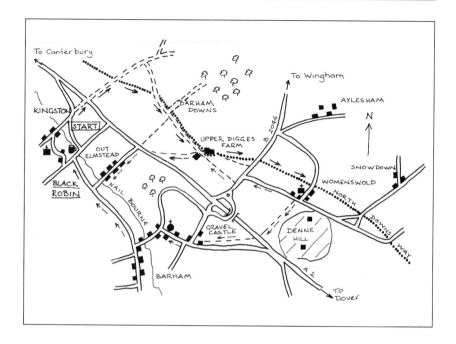

The National Trail is clearly marked here, as a path crossing a large field diagonally. At the far side it joins a wider track, along which it continues between the fields. At the next junction, where this track turns left, go straight on alongside a wooden fence. The Way is still clear and, all the while, the views should be over to the right, beyond the busy A2. In due course you reach Upper Digges Farm, behind a tall perimeter hedge on the left. Over to the right is a large bungalow. There is a junction of paths here. Do not go straight on. Instead turn left along a gravel track, keeping the perimeter hedge to your left, and then walk up a grassy track, through a gate and onwards into a field. Keep the farm buildings to your left.

At the far corner of these buildings bear right and follow a wide track running between fields. Arrow discs show the way. After going straight over the next junction of trackways, bear half-left along a path that cuts across a field diagonally. This brings you to the B2046. Cross over and continue along the bridleway opposite, which leads directly to Womenswold. This is where you leave the North Downs Way, by turning right down the road, through the village.

There are two routes back to Kingston, both starting from the T-junction at the southern end of Womenswold. The longer one includes

The village of Barham.

the village of Barham, another old and pretty settlement. This follows the bridleway signposted southwards (past Denne Hill) and then, across the A2, continues along a footpath to Gravel Castle, where the lane to Barham can be joined.

The shorter route leads westward to the B2046 (site of a hilltop beacon basket) and then, by way of a bridleway, back to Upper Digges Farm. From there follow the path downhill, diagonally across the field past the large bungalow mentioned earlier. This bungalow, incidentally, stands on the site of an old windmill, tragically burnt down in 1970. At the A2 walk alongside the fence for a few yards to the right before crossing over, to walk down Out Elmstead Lane. At the junction beyond Out Elmstead hamlet turn right for Kingston.

North Downs Way

The National Trail leaves Canterbury through the orchards southeast of the city centre. By lane and trackway it runs roughly parallel to the A2, through the village of Patrixbourne. From Womenswold it veers away from the A2, to skirt the villages once associated with the Kent Coalfield.

SHEPHERDSWELL
The Bell Inn

*F*rom *Woolage to Dover the North Downs Way continues across the broad chalk uplands, through an area once busy with coal mining. For the last 3 miles before the coast the National Trail follows the line of an old Roman road that linked Dover with Richborough, on Pegwell Bay. This circular walk includes a 2 mile stretch of the North Downs Way, crossing the landscaped Waldershare Park, famous for its beech, chestnut and lime trees. Waldershare House itself is a fine Classical mansion and, all around, the countryside boasts a pretty mixture of woods, orchards and fields of mixed farming.*

Shepherdswell, also known as Sibertswold, has two distinct parts: the western end around the railway station is largely Victorian in age, while to the east is the older centre around the village green and church.

The Bell Inn stands opposite the church facing this village green. It dates from the 18th century and now exhibits all the best attributes of a traditional English pub. There are low ceilings, plain walls hung with old pictures of the village, and a large brick fireplace where logs burn in winter months. The main bar room is sub-divided by a half-timbered partition and a dining area is separate. A pool table and dart board are both provided. The atmosphere is friendly, welcoming and cosy.

This is a Pubmaster house serving several real ales (such as Hancocks, Boddingtons and Tap and Spile), Blackthorn cider and a good house wine. Bar snacks include sandwiches, salads, ploughman's lunches and various 'with chips' meals; main dishes range from scampi, lasagne and meat pies to tikka and vegetable bakes. There should be something for everyone. All the food is well cooked and reasonably priced. Buffets and speciality meals can be prepared if pre-ordered.

Children are welcome and normal pub opening times are kept – except when all day opening occurs on days when demand requires. Telephone: 01304 830374.

- **HOW TO GET THERE:** Shepherdswell is 6 miles north-west of Dover, just a mile north of the A2. It can also be reached from the A256 via Eythorne.
- **PARKING:** There is a large pub car park and vehicles can also be left, here and there, around the village streets.
- **LENGTH OF THE WALK:** 4½ miles. Map OS Landranger 179 Canterbury (inn GR 262478). The paths and tracks are all well marked with signposts or arrow discs. However, a few have not worn well. There are many stiles to cross but the landscape is fairly level so no difficulties should be encountered.

THE WALK

The North Downs Way runs through the village and can be joined a short way from the church, to the left as you cross the village green from the Bell.

The green has an interesting information board. It seems that the original village name derived from the Saxon Sibert (a tribal chief) and 'wold' meaning a wood. Through the Middle Ages this became corrupted so that by the 19th century it was Shebberts Well. When the railway came in 1861 the station was called Shepherds Well. The church was rebuilt by the Victorians. From the late 19th century to the 1930s Shepherdswell grew steadily, largely as a result of nearby coal mining, but today the village is mainly a dormitory settlement for Dover.

 A signpost points down a path that runs beside the churchyard to a stile. The route is very clear and regularly marked by arrow discs.

85

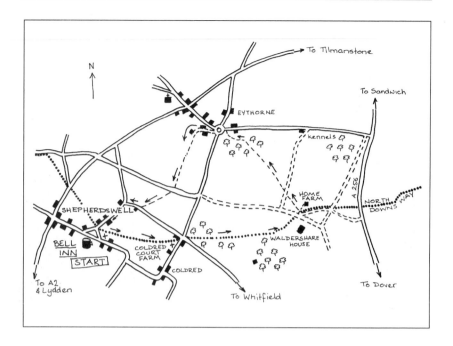

It runs down the edge of a paddock, alongside a hedgerow and then, half-left, across two large fields diagonally. Beyond a belt of trees, which shows the course of an old mineral railway, the Way continues in the same direction over two more fields and stiles, to emerge at the road near Coldred Court Farm and the picturesque Coldred church.

From the crossroads here the North Downs Way continues north-eastwards, in almost a straight line. It runs through trees, over a field, through a small wood and then diagonally across two large fields to the corner of distant woodland. The brick-built belvedere, dating from 1725, can be seen over to the right. This square-towered folly once dominated the landscaped parkland hereabouts but now stands sadly forlorn. Beyond the woodland continue across the next field aiming to the left of Waldershare House which, by now, has come into view. Cross over a gravel track to reach a stile and a lane, where you turn right.

Leaving the North Downs Way opposite the vehicular entrance to the west front of Waldershare House, turn left through the gate and walk beside the avenue of trees towards Home Farm.

The way back begins along a right of way which is not very clear, but is very straight and well served by stiles and arrow discs. Just before reaching Home Farm turn left and walk north-westwards, diagonally

The picturesque church at Coldred.

across a large field dotted with mature trees. Cross over the gravel lane that leads to the handsome kennels building and continue in the same direction across two more fields downhill towards distant woodland. There, amongst the trees, a large step stile leads to a clear path. This runs attractively along a belt of woodland, eventually to emerge beside some garden fences on the road at Eythorne.

Across the Eythorne roundabout walk down Flax Court Lane, a gravel track that passes a number of houses and then turns sharply left immediately before the last residence. Now (slightly narrower) it heads straight on, between trees and fields, eventually to meet a road. Cross this and continue along the footpath opposite that goes, half-right, diagonally across a very large field. Shepherdswell is soon reached. Turn right and left along the village streets to reach the Bell.

North Downs Way

The National Trail turns south when it reaches the village of Ashley, 1 mile beyond Waldershare House. Following an old Roman road it continues mostly along a byway that is now also used by the White Cliffs Country Trail. The North Downs Way enters Dover beside Connaught Park.

STANFORD

The Drum Inn

From Dover to Stowting the North Downs Way runs along the coastline, over the White Cliffs to East Wear Bay, and then inland behind Folkestone. As much as possible it keeps to the crest of the chalk escarpment but the use of existing footpaths determines a fairly circuitous route. A prehistoric track once ran along the base of the scarp slope, from Dover to Wye, and it was this which was probably used by medieval pilgrims travelling over from Europe. This circular walk includes a 1½ mile stretch of the North Downs Way, as it skirts the top of the hills above the pretty village of Postling. There are wide views along the coastline towards Dungeness and beyond.

Stanford is a long narrow village with a small bell-towered church, a brick-built windmill which has seen better days, and a pleasant mixture of houses. At the southern end is an M20 motorway bridge and a railway station, at the northern end is the Drum Inn.

This was built in the early 18th century and takes its name from a military connection, the Duke of Marlborough having stationed some of his troops here for recruitment purposes. Later in the same century, it is said, the Drum Inn also became a watchtower for Revenue men in their hunt for smugglers.

Today the place is more peaceful although, at times, no less bustling. It is popular with locals and tourists alike and is especially welcoming to families. The large garden contains various children's play things. Inside there is a large open-plan bar room at the front and a quieter lounge beyond. All is dark and cosy with low beamed ceilings, bare brick pillars and plain plaster walls decorated with pictures and brassware.

This is a Greene King house serving various real ales (all Greene King brands plus guest beers), draught ciders and wines. The menu of homemade dishes is suitably wide to suit all tastes and pockets. From sandwiches, ploughman's lunches and jacket potatoes the range rises to such items as scampi and chips, steak and kidney pie, lasagne, spaghetti bolognese and curry. Vegetarians can also make special orders to match their requirements.

Normal pub opening times are kept. Telephone: 01303 812125.

- **HOW TO GET THERE:** Stanford is 6 miles west of Folkestone and 8 miles south-east of Ashford. It is close to Junction 11 on the M20 and the B2068 road to Canterbury.
- **PARKING:** There is a large pub car park. Vehicles can also be left along the roadsides nearby, provided no obstruction is caused.
- **LENGTH OF THE WALK:** 4½ miles. Map OS Landranger 189 Ashford (inn GR 129384). The route is well signposted throughout although the paths are not always very clear. Some steep gradients are encountered and numerous stiles. However, this is not a difficult walk and should be enjoyed at leisure.

THE WALK

Turn left outside the Drum Inn and walk northwards along the B2068. This is called Stone Street and follows the alignment of an old Roman road that linked Lympne (then a coastal settlement) with Canterbury. Shortly before the line of pylons turn right along a grassy track, 50 yards before reaching a house. This track, although sometimes overgrown, is very clear as it crosses a stream and proceeds through a small wood. The Downs, over to the left, are dominated by the telecommunications tower at Etchinghill but the view is pleasant nonetheless. Beyond the trees the trackway runs along the edge of a field, with a wire fence on the left.

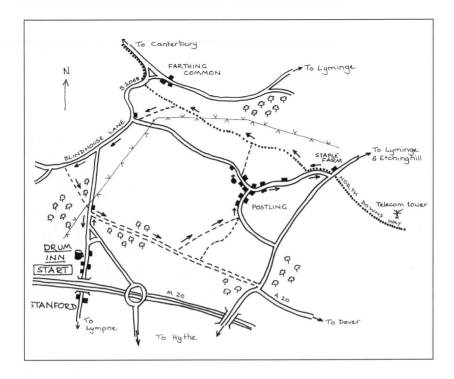

Soon you reach a point where one footpath joins from the right (stile) and another close by joins from the left (stile). Follow the latter, northwards.

In fact, the path to Postling is not wonderfully clear as it crosses a number of fields. But there are stiles to aim for and the route is fairly straight. Another right of way crosses the fields further east, from the trackway to Postling, and this could be easier to follow. Both footpaths end at the road south of the village. A 1 mile road walk now follows through Postling, bearing right at the junction and climbing the Downs to the junction near Staple Farm.

The North Downs Way is joined across the stile on the left, at the road junction near Staple Farm on top of the hill. Along this next stretch the National Trail is simply a grassy path running across pasture fields. At first it runs alongside the hedgerow, parallel to the road you have just walked along, but soon it turns right to climb up to the skyline. For the next mile you follow it as it skirts the edge of the slopes that dip down to Postling.

The Way is not always clear but regular arrow discs show the

The pretty village of Postling.

direction. In due course you walk under a line of pylons and, after a dip and a climb, reach a stile leading into a large field. Leave the North Downs Way here and turn left, before the stile.

The way back begins with a descent of the scarp slope. At the corner of the wire fence that you have followed for a short distance, bear half-right. The path goes down the steep slope at an angle, eventually to a stile half-hidden in the bottom hedgerow. Beyond this is the road where you turn right. At the main junction turn left down the B2068 and then, where the road forks after 400 yards, right down Blindhouse Lane. The footpath required will be found on the left where this road bends right. It crosses two large fields diagonally, eventually to meet the B2068 under the line of pylons. Once back on the main road turn right for the short walk southwards to the Drum Inn.

North Downs Way

The National Trail, from Dover to Folkestone, is now sadly dominated by the busy A20 and the Channel Tunnel rail connections. It weaves its way along the clifftop and then westwards to Etchinghill accompanied by the Saxon Shore Way, a designated coastal route from Gravesend to Hastings. The way used by foreign pilgrims, travelling to Canterbury, is now lost under modern development. However, it can be traced west of Postling along existing roads along the base of the scarp slope below Cobb's Hill.

HASTINGLEIGH
The Bowl Inn

From Stowting to Wye the North Downs Way continues along the crest of the chalk hills. Beyond Wye, where it crosses the Great Stour river, it climbs the slope to Boughton Lees. Here it joins the route to Canterbury, closing the 'Kent Loop'. The way of the pilgrims, coming up from the Channel, ran along the bottom of the scarp slope. This circular walk includes a 2 mile stretch of the North Downs Way as it meanders through the Wye Nature Reserve and over Wye Downs. There are wonderful views from here and the countryside all around is rich in downland wildlife.

Hastingleigh is a pretty, quiet little village nestling in the midst of some of the loveliest countryside in Kent. It has a pond, a collection of old cottages and a little general store, all shaded by a range of fine mature trees. The Bowl Inn stands at the western end.

This freehouse is the kind of village local that is, sadly, disappearing. It is old without being 'olde worlde', it is traditional without being twee. It has a friendly, homely atmosphere and a welcome that is unpretentious. There is a 'tap room' with a pool table and two other small rooms, one with a dart board. The ceilings are fairly low and the walls are sparsely hung with pictures and plates. At the back is a large cottage garden with island beds full of flowers, scattered pots and a mixed collection of tables and chairs. In summer months, especially, the aspect is a delight.

Various real ales are served including Ind Coope, Adnams and Ansells and the cider is Scrumpy Jack. There is also the usual choice of wines, lagers and stouts. Bar snacks only are offered but the range of these is good, including hot and cold items. There are sandwiches, salads and ploughman's lunches; pizzas, curries and pasta dishes; ham, egg and chips or omelettes. No one should go hungry.

Normal pub opening times are kept, although one lunchtime per week is excluded. Children are welcome. Telephone: 01233 750354.

- **HOW TO GET THERE:** Hastingleigh is 6 miles north-east of Ashford and 10 miles north-west of Folkestone. It can be reached from Junction 10 on the M20 or from the A28 via Wye.
- **PARKING:** There is a pub car park. Vehicles can also be left here and there around the village.
- **LENGTH OF THE WALK:** 4½ miles. Map OS Landranger 189 Ashford (inn GR 095449). All the paths and tracks used are well worn and well marked by signposts or arrow discs. Numerous stiles are encountered but there should be no difficulty due to terrain since the route is generally level.

THE WALK

From outside the Bowl Inn turn left and walk westwards away from the village. Ignoring the lane on the right, continue along the road to the crossroads where you go straight over. About 300 yards further on is another junction but this one is where a byway crosses, each lane being a 'no through road' for traffic. Turn left here and walk to Cold Blow Farm, where the tarmac ends. Just beyond the farmbuildings is the North Downs Way, a stile either side of the track marking its route. Turn right here and follow the direction indicated by the arrow signs.

The National Trail here is a grassy path across open pasture fields. It follows the top edge of the scarp slope and affords a wonderful view to the left, in a sweep of country from the Weald to Romney

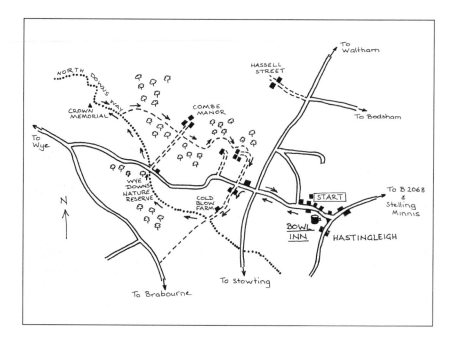

Marsh. On the far side of the first field a stile and gate lead you through into an area of access land status. Continue alongside the hedgerow to another stile, after which turn left, then right, around the outer edge of a fenced-in field. Beyond another stile you continue in the same direction, ignoring the gate on the left that leads to a track going downhill.

By this time you have entered the Wye Downs Nature Reserve, now under the control of English Nature. It is a lovely spot and you should take your time walking across the open hilltop.

Keeping to the line of a wire fence, and over another stile, you skirt the top rim of the deep coombe known as the Devil's Kneading Trough. There is a car park and restaurant, out of sight, up to your right but you continue straight on to a gate. Thereafter the North Downs Way curves its way through woodland to meet the road at an angle. Across this it runs in the same direction, now as a bridleway alongside a fence.

Follow this route all the way to the end of the ridge, where you can look down upon the Crown memorial. This was carved in the chalk hillside in 1902 by students of nearby Wye college, to mark the coronation of Edward VII. The village of Wye can clearly be seen below.

The route back to Hastingleigh begins along the North Downs Way,

Wye.

retracing your steps for about 400 yards. Turn left to follow the footpath that crosses a field and winds downhill through woodland. Beyond the trees continue along the edge of a large field, descending beside the wood to a tarmac farm lane. Cross straight over and continue alongside a fence and then beside more woodland, which is to your right. In the bottom corner turn left, up along the edge of the same field, to a stile and then bear right to climb through a group of trees.

Beyond these walk up to a gate and stile, after which contour above and around a large farmstead along a clear track. On the far side ascend to the top corner of the field where a stile under some trees leads to a path that connects with a gravel track. Turn left along this. Soon you will reach a road that you should recognise, since you were here near the start of the walk. Turn left along the road that leads eastwards back to the Bowl Inn.

North Downs Way

The National Trail crosses the narrow valley, where stands the village of Stowting, and then regains height above Brabourne. From there it continues along the top of the Downs all the way to Wye, where it descends to the Great Stour river. The way of the pilgrims is now used by modern roads, running north of Brabourne and Brook.

95

INFORMATION AND ACCOMMODATION

If you are planning to walk the Pilgrims' Way or the North Downs Way in a linear fashion, then you will find it sensible to refer to books which specifically cater for the long distance walker. Those books which can be recommended include the following three. *The National Trail Guide - North Downs Way* by Neil Curtis (Aurum Press) is a detailed guide with maps and directional information; *North Downs Way - A Practical Handbook* (Kent County Council) has general information about facilities along the way, including accommodation; *A Guide to the Pilgrims' Way and North Downs Way* by Christopher John Wright (Constable) describes both routes and is particularly good on history and background information.

Various guides, leaflets and information packs are available from the following. They can also give general advice about facilities, transport and accommodation to be found along the Pilgrims' Way and North Downs Way.

Countryside Commission, John Dower House, Crescent Place, Cheltenham, Gloucestershire GL50 3RA.

The Ramblers' Association, 1-5 Wandsworth Road, London SW8 2XX.

Byways and Bridleways Trust, 9 Queen Anne's Gate, London SW1H 9BH.

Long Distance Walkers' Association, 29 Appledown Road, Alresford, Hampshire SO24 9ND.

Surrey County Council, Highways Department, County Hall, Kingston upon Thames, Surrey KT1 2DN.

Kent County Council, North Downs Way Office, Springfield, Maidstone, Kent ME14 2LQ.

Southern England Tourist Board, 40 Chamberlayne Road, Eastleigh, Hampshire SO5 5JH. Tel: 01703 620006. South East England Tourist Board, The Old Brew House, Warwick Park, Tunbridge Wells, Kent TN2 5TU. Tel: 01892 540766.